Baylor Scott & White Health's approach to achieving the Triple Aim is both innovative and proven. This book provides the practical information and real-life examples that individuals and organizations will find extraordinarily useful to improve and enhance care in their settings...it is a "must have" for anyone interested in maximizing patient safety.

Beth Mancini, RN, PhD, NE-BC, FAHA, ANEF, FAAN
Professor, Associate Dean, and Chair Undergraduate Nursing Programs
The University of Texas at Arlington College of Nursing and Health Innovation
Baylor Professor for Healthcare Research
Past President, The Society for Simulation in Healthcare

Baylor Scott & White Health is way out in front of the pack in their approach to safety, using a true systems approach, embedding PhD-level human factors engineers in their safety program, and creating a robust training program for their safety teams in the science of safety. This is a system worth watching.

Rollin J. (Terry) Fairbanks, MD, MS
Director, National Center for Human Factors in Healthcare
Director, Simulation Training & Education Lab (MedStar SiTEL)
MedStar Institute for Innovation, MedStar Health
Associate Professor of Emergency Medicine, Georgetown University

There is no better way to evaluate an approach than to introduce it. Baylor Scott & White Health has done this with STEEEP to great effect. There are lessons aplenty in this excellent publication from Baylor Scott & White Health.

Peter Carter
Chief Executive Officer
International Society for Quality in Health Care

Jan Compton and her colleagues at Baylor Scott & White Health have produced a valuable compendium reflecting the intentional efforts to systematically improve care across their health system. This intentional work has resulted in a considerably safer care environment for both patients and the people providing care.

Michael Leonard, MD
Managing Partner
Safe & Reliable Healthcare LLC
Adjunct Professor of Medicine
Duke University School of Medicine

Measuring and reducing patient harm are central to delivering safe and reliable healthcare and yet, based on the evidence, remains a challenge for most. STEEEP care created an even higher standard by pioneering preventable risk, one of many ways in which Baylor Scott & White Health (BSWH) has proven a trailblazer in high reliability. This book is a gift to the field and demonstrates how BSWH will remain a leader in this next generation of patient care.

Drew Ladner, MBA, MA
Chairman & CEO
Pascal Metrics

In this book, Baylor Scott & White Health has once again illustrated why it's a leader in the field of medicine. If every hospital in America was as direct in its goal to reduce patient harm, we could cut preventable deaths by a significant number. While no one has all of the answers to solving the patient safety problem in this country, Baylor Scott & White Health is leading the way to reach zero preventable deaths. We thank them for their commitment to patients.

Laura Batz Townsend
Co-Founder & President
Louise H. Batz Patient Safety Foundation

Baylor Scott & White Health provides practical examples and approaches to excellence in patient safety in *Achieving Safe Health Care*. Each page holds ideas that any system can implement. Further, Baylor Scott & White Health provides detailed measurement of its improvements utilizing the STEEEP program.

Kristin M. Jenkins, JD, MBA, FACHE
President
Dallas-Fort Worth Hospital Council Foundation
Senior Vice President
Dallas-Fort Worth Hospital Council

ACHIEVING SAFE HEALTH CARE

Delivery of Safe Patient Care at Baylor Scott & White Health

Jan Compton, MS-HCAD, BSN, RN, CPHQ

With Kathleen M. Richter, MBA, MS, MFA

Foreword by David C. Classen, MD, MS

CRC Press
Taylor & Francis Group
Boca Raton London New York

CRC Press is an imprint of the
Taylor & Francis Group, an **informa** business
A PRODUCTIVITY PRESS BOOK

CRC Press
Taylor & Francis Group
6000 Broken Sound Parkway NW, Suite 300
Boca Raton, FL 33487-2742

First issued in paperback 2021

ISBN 13: 978-1-03-209816-6 (pbk)
ISBN 13: 978-1-4987-3239-0 (hbk)

Library of Congress Cataloging-in-Publication Data

Compton, Jan, author.
  Achieving safe health care : delivery of safe patient care at Baylor Scott & White Health / Jan Compton.
  p. ; cm.
  Includes bibliographical references and index.
  ISBN 978-1-4987-3239-0
  I. Title.
  [DNLM: 1. Baylor Scott & White Health. 2. Hospital Administration--methods. 3. Quality of Health Care. 4. Hospitals--standards. 5. Patient-Centered Care. WX 153]
  RA971
  362.11068--dc23   2015023290

Visit the Taylor & Francis Web site at
http://www.taylorandfrancis.com

and the CRC Press Web site at
http://www.crcpress.com

Contents

Foreword

More than fifteen years after the Institute of Medicine report *To Err Is Human*, patient safety remains a significant problem for the U.S. health care system and, more emphatically, for American patients who still suffer high rates of harm. Recent studies have estimated that more than 400,000 lives are lost each year because of safety problems in American hospitals, making safety the third leading cause of death in the United States.[1] In addition, more than six million injuries may occur to patients undergoing inpatient care in the United States. Yes, there have been improvements in safety—hospital mortality rates have declined along with certain types of safety problems such as central line–associated blood stream infections and ventilator–associated pneumonia. However, the startling figures mentioned previously tell a bigger story, that many serious patient safety problems remain to be addressed. Many health care professionals well aware of these safety problems closely monitor and follow family members and loved ones who get hospitalized. The recent publication of surgeon-specific complication rates with huge variation has only fueled public interest and concern about the safety of care. The rapid rise of high-deductible health plans now means that patients are covering a larger financial burden from these injuries.

Given these many current challenges in improving patient safety, what are the greatest opportunities in moving forward in improving patient safety? As other high-risk industries have learned, it starts with leadership completely committing itself, not just to the talk but to the walk as well. It continues with creating a culture of safety throughout the organization that touches everyone, even those not directly involved in patient care. It requires a commitment to safety culture that overrides a focus on productivity—allowing health care workers to "stop the line" if a situation not only is unsafe but also even looks unsafe. It demands thinking ahead in safety using the principles of human factors to redesign the health care process. It cannot work without the safe adoption and broad use of technology and it must also include a degree of collaboration and teamwork heretofore not seen in health care. And finally, it can never be successful without the deep involvement of patients and families. For a health care organization to truly achieve safe and highly reliable care, all these things must be working as a well-conducted symphony. Given the complexity of the adaptive organism that we call a hospital or a health system, this has not yet arrived in American health care. However, the blueprint for just this transformation is outlined in great detail in this book, *Achieving Safe Health Care: Delivery of Safe Patient Care at Baylor Scott & White Health*, which outlines what this symphony will look like.

Over the last two decades, Baylor Scott & White Health (BSWH) has been putting together this organizational blueprint for safer and higher reliable care. It is built on top of leadership commitment and structure and aligned incentives to carry it out. Beginning with an integrated plan for enhancing quality of care called STEEEP (safe, timely, effective, efficient, equitable, patient-centered care), BSWH began by reducing preventable deaths, then reducing preventable injuries, and finally reducing preventable risk. In essence, unlike so many other patient safety plans, this is a plan with a proven track record. It is also a plan that has benefited from more than a decade of education, training, innovation, and testing. Although BSWH heavily uses successful approaches from other organizations, in many cases, innovative approaches to safety had to be developed and innovated by BSWH. This book is replete with examples of these important safety innovations. From the novel and aggressive use of human factors expertise to redesigning health care processes or technology design or use, to the reinvention of surgical checklists with real-life pragmatic workflows, to the development of a unique BSWH safety culture assessment tool, to the use of Swaddle teams to support health care workers who disclose patient safety problems to patients, to the deep involvement of patients and families in all aspects of the BSWH safety programs including the creation of patient white boards and the safety huddle approach to instill principles of high reliability at the frontlines of care, to the development of a new model of root cause analysis called the Cardiac Surgery Phase of Care Mortality Analysis, to the development and use of an all-cause harm measure based on the Institute for Healthcare Improvement Global Trigger Tool, this book abounds with innovations beyond the ones mentioned here.

Other industries such as aviation and nuclear power have shown us that there is safety in numbers: Achieving safe and highly reliable performance requires an organization that operates on a daily basis with the principles of high reliability, continually measures its safety performance, always looks for opportunities to improve, and is hypervigilant about safety events, risks, near-misses, and those safety problems that have not yet been recognized. This will require health care organizations to move from a focus on a series of specific safety initiatives such as reducing medication errors to an overall organizational approach and plan to achieve this world of highly reliable and safe care. This book is that plan and should be required reading for any health care leader who wants to transform his or her organizational approach and performance in patient safety. Indeed, this book may become the blueprint for how to deliver the safest care possible, something that remains a great challenge as well as a great opportunity for the US health care system.

David C. Classen, MD, MS
Chief Medical Information Officer, Pascal Metrics
Associate Professor of Medicine, University of Utah
Salt Lake City, Utah

Reference

1. James, J.T., A new, evidence-based estimate of patient harms associated with hospital care. *Journal of Patient Safety*, 2013. **9**(3): pp. 122–28. Available from http://journals.lww.com/journalpatientsafety/Fulltext/2013/09000/A_New _Evidence_based_Estimate_of_Patient_Harms.2.aspx.

Acknowledgments

Each day, I am privileged to work with more than 35,000 employees of Baylor Scott & White Health (BSWH) who dedicate themselves to delivering the BSWH vision "to be the most trusted name in giving and receiving *safe*, quality, compassionate health care." They do this by operationalizing the STEEEP quality framework—health care that is safe, timely, effective, efficient, equitable, and patient centered. Everything we do as a health care organization starts with the safe delivery of care.

I am both committed and excited to be on this mission to achieve safe care with an organization passionate about delivering exemplary care to the patients we serve. This book provides details on the strategies and tactics we as a health care system have implemented to achieve safe health care. More importantly, this book provides stories from the frontline about how engagement with and commitment to patient safety prevent errors from occurring. It is truly an honor to be able to share this journey on behalf of the BSWH team. The culture and dedication exhibited by each employee are what make BSWH the best place to give and receive care. Health care is very competitive, but when the topic is patient safety, hospitals and health care systems should work together and share how to achieve the best possible outcomes in the journey to safer care. It is my hope that this book provides insight into making health care safer.

I want to thank those leaders across BSWH who mentored me when I was a nurse beginning my journey and those who have provided wisdom and leadership to define the leader I have become.

In addition, I am appreciative of Dr. Paul Convery, Nanette Myers, Kathleen Richter, Hilda Williams, and Alyssa Zarro, who provided editorial support during the production of this book, and to Dr. Don Kennerly, for building the foundation for the patient safety program in 2005 and allowing me to take that vision and continue to build a robust patient safety program. Thank you for those in the Office of Patient Safety who share my passion for this very important work. Last, thank you to Dr. David Ballard for giving me the opportunity to tell our story.

Author

Jan Compton, MS-HCAD, BSN, RN, CPHQ, is vice president of patient safety and chief patient safety officer for Baylor Scott & White Health (BSWH), the largest not-for-profit health care system in Texas, which includes 46 hospitals, more than 800 patient care sites, 5800 affiliated physicians, more than 35,000 employees, and the Scott & White Health Plan. In this role, she is responsible for overseeing the health care system's efforts to develop and implement evidence-based patient safety practices intended to help the organization pursue its vision of "no preventable deaths, no preventable injuries, and no preventable risk." Jan's passion for patient safety is clearly demonstrated as she leads by influence the BSWH programs to reduce inpatient mortality, promotes an organizational culture conducive to the development of patient safety innovations, and guides employees in the adoption of patient safety values. Her plan is to operationalize patient safety goals and processes across all BSWH facilities.

Jan dreamed of becoming a nurse since early childhood. She lost her mother at an early age but has very vivid memories of her mother dressed in her white nursing uniform, smiling and always with a compassionate, caring heart no matter how tired she was. Jan's adoptive parents encouraged her to apply herself in school and pursue her dreams. The values instilled while she was growing up were honesty, integrity, and compassion for others. These are the values that she lives by in both her professional and personal life.

Jan earned her bachelor of science in nursing as well as her master of science in health care administration from the University of Texas at Arlington. She has more than 30 years of nursing experience at BSWH. Jan began her nursing career in critical care, where her passion for quality and patient safety first started. Jan's experience also includes previous roles as nursing supervisor; cardiovascular care coordinator; and director of health care improvement, care coordination, risk management, patient safety, and guest relations for the Baylor Jack and Jane Hamilton Heart and Vascular Hospital. In her former role as director of patient safety for Baylor Health Care System (BHCS), she was responsible for the oversight, growth, and development of the BHCS Office of Patient Safety direct-report employees and facility-level direct-report employees, evaluations, and budget. Under Jan's leadership, the BSWH patient safety assessment program has spread and is now being implemented across the entire health care system to ensure a safe culture for our patients and staff.

Jan is a Certified Professional in Healthcare Quality. She is a member of the North Texas Association for Healthcare Quality, member and past chair for the Patient Safety and Quality Committee for the Dallas-Fort Worth Hospital Council, and a member of the North Texas Health Information and Quality Collaborative for the Dallas-Fort Worth Hospital Council.

Contributors

Toni Akers, BSN, MBA, RN-BC
Regional Director, Clinical
 Informatics
Baylor Scott & White Health-North
Dallas, Texas

**David Ballard, MD, MSPH, PhD,
FACP**
Chief Quality Officer
President, STEEEP Global Institute
Baylor Scott & White Health
Dallas, Texas

**Dora Bradley, PhD, RN-BC,
FAAN**
Chief Clinical & Patient Learning
 Officer
Baylor Scott & White Health
Dallas, Texas

Cindy Cassity, RN, BSN
Manager of Patient Safety
Baylor University Medical Center
 at Dallas
Dallas, Texas

**Tammy Cohen, BS, PharmD, MS,
FASHP, FTSHP**
System Vice President, Pharmacy
 Services
Baylor Scott & White Health
Dallas, Texas

**William Cooksey, RN, MBA,
FACHE**
Director of Quality, Cardiovascular
 Services
Baylor Scott & White Health
Dallas, Texas

Karen Copeland, RN, CPHRM
Patient Safety Measurement
 Specialist
Baylor Scott & White Health-North
Dallas, Texas

**Marsha Cox, RN, MSN, PhD,
MBA**
Director of Health Care
 Improvement
Baylor Scott & White Health
Dallas, Texas

Brenda Davis, RN, BSN, MBA
Chief Operating Officer & Chief
  Nursing Officer, College Station
  Region
Baylor Scott & White Health
College Station, Texas

Chris Felton, RN
Director of Clinical Improvement
HealthTexas Provider Network
Dallas, Texas

John Foster, PharmD, MBA
Director of Pharmacy
Baylor Medical Center at McKinney
McKinney, Texas

Richard Gilder, RN, BSN, MS, CNOR, BCNI
Data Scientist-Nursing Analysis
  Champion
Baylor Scott & White Health
Dallas, Texas

Becky Hardie, BSN, RNC-OB, MS HCAD, NEA-BC
Vice President of Administration
Baylor All Saints Medical Center
and
Vice President of Women's and
  Infants' Service Line
Baylor Scott & White Health-North
Fort Worth, Texas

Lisa Havens, JD
Senior Vice President System Risk
  Officer
Baylor Scott & White Health
Temple, Texas

Molly Hicks, RN, BSN, MSN
Director of Patient Safety
Baylor Scott & White Health-North
Dallas, Texas

Steve Hoeft, MBA, PMP
Chief of Operations Excellence
Baylor Scott & White Health
Temple, Texas

Jason Jennings, FACHE
Chief Executive Officer, College
  Station Region
Baylor Scott & White Health
College Station, Texas

Alan Jones, MD
Director of Orthopedic Trauma
Program Director, Orthopedic
  Residency Program
Baylor University Medical Center at
  Dallas
Dallas, Texas

Amy Kent, RN, BSN
Manager of Patient Safety
HealthTexas Provider Network
Dallas, Texas

Alice Kern-Kirby, RN, MBA
Director of Nursing
Baylor Regional Medical Center at
  Plano
Plano, Texas

Terry Long, RN, MSN, CPHQ
Vice President, Office of the Chief
    Quality Officer
Baylor Scott & White Health
Temple, Texas

Will Long, MIS, CISSP, CPHIMSS
Vice President Information Services
Baylor Scott & White Health
Dallas, Texas

Rosemary Luquire, RN, PhD,
FAAN, NEA-BC
Chief Nurse Executive
Baylor Scott & White Health
Dallas, Texas

Jeffrey McKenzie
Director of Systems & Support
Baylor Scott & White Health-North
Dallas, Texas

Scott Meril, MD
Patient Safety Physician Champion
Baylor Medical Center at Garland
Garland, Texas

Alan Miller, MD, PHD
Director
Baylor Charles A. Sammons Cancer
    Center at Dallas
and
Chief of Oncology
Baylor Scott & White Health-North
Dallas, Texas

Donna Montgomery, RN-BC,
BSN, MBA
Vice President of Nursing
    Informatics & Clinical Excellence
Baylor Scott & White Health-North
Dallas, Texas

Anthony Morgan, RN, BSN, MSN
Corporate Director, Electronic
    Health Record Applications
Baylor Scott & White Health-North
Dallas, Texas

Cindy Murray, MBA, MHA, RN,
CNOR, CENP
Chief Nursing Officer & Chief
    Operating Officer
Baylor Scott & White Medical
    Center at Waxahachie
Waxahachie, Texas

Therese Nelson, RN, CPHRM
Clinical Risk Manager, Patient
    Safety Officer, & Compliance
    Liaison
Baylor Medical Center at Garland
Garland, Texas

Michael Pittman, FACHE, RN
Chief Operating Officer & Chief
    Nursing Officer
Scott & White Hospital-Brenham
Brenham, Texas

Judy Prescott, RN, BSN, CIC
Director of Infection Prevention &
    Control
Baylor Scott & White Health
Dallas, Texas

C. Adam Probst, PhD
Senior Human Factors Specialist
Baylor Scott & White Health
Dallas, Texas

Michael Ramsay, MD
Chairman, Department of
  Anesthesiology & Pain
  Management
Baylor University Medical Center
  at Dallas
Dallas, Texas

Dennis Raymer, BS
System Director, Operations
  Excellence
Baylor Scott & White Health
Temple, Texas

Susan Roden, MSN, RN, HACP
Director of Quality & Patient Safety
Scott & White Hospital-Brenham
Brenham, Texas

**Cherie Sajewski, MHA, BSN, RN,
CPHQ, HACP**
Director of Quality Management
  Program
Scott & White Hospital-College
  Station
College Station, Texas

Margaret Saldaña, MPH, RHIA
Manager of Patient Safety
Baylor Scott & White Health-North
Dallas, Texas

Joseph H. Schneider, MD, MBA
Vice President of Clinical
  Informatics & Chief Medical
  Information Officer
Baylor Scott & White Health-North
Dallas, Texas

Abeezar Shipchandler, MD, FACP
Internal Medicine/Hospitalist
Baylor Regional Medical Center at
  Plano
and
Physician Clinical Informatics
  Leader
Baylor Scott & White Health
Plano, Texas

Christopher Shutts, MBA, CSSBB
Vice President, STEEEP Care
  Improvement Education
Baylor Scott & White Health
Dallas, Texas

William Sutker, MD
Director of Medical Education &
  Patient Safety Officer
Baylor University Medical Center at
  Dallas
Dallas, Texas

**Remy Tolentino, MSN, RN,
NEA-BC**
Vice President, Nursing Workforce
  & Leadership Development
and
Project Director, Deerbrook Grant
  on Improving Geriatric Care
Baylor Scott & White Health-North
Dallas, Texas

Jason Trahan, PharmD
Director of Pharmacy-Medication
  Safety
Baylor Scott & White Health
Dallas, Texas

Sharon Tucker, MD, FAAFP
Family Physician
Baylor Family Health Center at
  Mesquite
and
Medical Director, Patient Safety
HealthTexas Provider Network
Mesquite, Texas

David Watson, BS, RPh
Director of Pharmacy Informatics
Baylor Scott & White Health
Dallas, Texas

Robert Watson, MD, MMM, CPE
Medical Director
Baylor Scott & White Quality
  Alliance
and
Physician Leader, Women's Health
  Service Line
Baylor Scott & White Health-North
Fort Worth, Texas

Holly Winchester, BSN, RN-BC
Manager, Orders Management &
  Workflow
Baylor Scott & White Health-North
Dallas, Texas

Yan Xiao, PHD
Director of Human Factors &
  Patient Safety Science
Baylor Scott & White Health
Dallas, Texas

**Annabelle Zakarian, MSN, RN,
CVRN, NE-BC**
Director of Health Care
  Improvement, Risk Management,
  Patient Safety, & Cardiovascular
  Outcomes
Baylor Hamilton Heart and
  Vascular Hospital
Dallas, Texas

Introduction

Patient safety has always been a guiding principle of health care delivery for both Baylor Health Care System (BHCS) and Scott & White Healthcare (SWH), which were each founded over a century ago. When the two health care systems joined on October 1, 2013, to form Baylor Scott & White Health (BSWH), the largest not-for-profit health care system in Texas, organizational leaders supported a commitment to patient safety in the BSWH vision "to be the most trusted name in giving and receiving safe, quality, compassionate health care." To achieve this vision, BSWH embraces its mission "to serve all people by providing personalized health and wellness through exemplary care, education and research as a Christian ministry of healing," as well as its organizational values of integrity, servanthood, teamwork, excellence, innovation, and stewardship (see Figure I.1).

What Is STEEEP Care?

In addition to its vision, mission, and values, BSWH is committed to the delivery of care that is STEEEP® (safe, timely, effective, efficient, equitable, and patient centered) (Ballard et al. 2014). First described by the Institute of Medicine (IOM) (Corrigan et al. 2001), STEEEP care is

- Safe: avoiding injury to patients from care that is intended to help them, without accidental error or inadvertent exposure
- Timely: reducing waits and harmful delays impacting smooth flow of care
- Effective: providing services based on scientific knowledge to all who could benefit and refraining from providing services to those not likely to benefit (avoiding overuse and underuse)

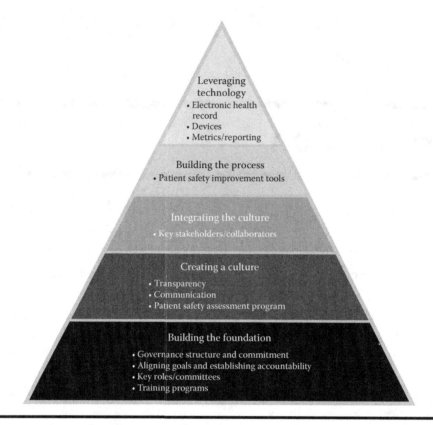

Figure I.1   Patient safety framework for achieving safe health care.

■ Efficient: using resources to achieve best value by reducing waste and reducing production and administrative costs
■ Equitable: providing care that does not vary in quality according to personal characteristics, such as gender, income, ethnicity, location
■ Patient centered: providing care that is respectful of and responsive to individual patient preference, needs, and values

   Imagining the analogy of climbing a mountain, BSWH leaders created and trademarked the STEEEP acronym in 2000 to convey the challenge of transforming the current health care delivery system to one exemplified by the elements of STEEEP care (Ballard et al. 2004).

Journey to STEEEP Care

Achieving STEEEP care is not an endpoint, but a journey. Traveling this path requires a commitment to continuous quality improvement from the highest levels of leadership as well as the development of five components of health care delivery: administration and governance, clinical leadership, quality programs and expertise, data and analytics, and accreditation (Ballard 2015). The STEEEP Quality Journey is portrayed in Figure I.2 in the context of these five components of health care delivery.

What Is Safe Care?

As defined by the IOM, safe care is care that avoids injury to patients from care that is intended to help them, without accidental error or inadvertent exposure. Like STEEEP care, safe care is a journey. It can be depicted along a continuum from no preventable deaths to no preventable injuries to no preventable risk (Figure I.3).

Achieving no preventable deaths requires answering questions such as the following: What is a preventable death? How do we know whether a death could have been prevented? How do we determine when a patient is critically ill and death may occur within weeks but not necessarily that day? Could a patient's life have been prolonged a few more days or weeks? Some deaths (such as for patients in hospice care) are expected, and comfort care and support may be the most appropriate treatment for these patients. How should a safety program impact these patients? For injuries, similar questions arise: What is a preventable injury? How can we measure preventable injuries accurately and learn from these events? Finally, how do we define and measure preventable risk? This book will address these and other questions relevant to designing, implementing, and measuring the impact of an organizational patient safety program. It will describe the patient safety journey of the BSWH organization and will highlight many of the key strategies, processes, and tools that have resulted in safer care.

Culture, Processes, and Technology

Strategies to achieve safe care can be broadly categorized into the areas of culture, processes, and technology. To instill a culture of safety throughout the organization, it is essential to perform cultural self-assessments; align the culture with the organization's vision, mission, and values; and foster an organizational environment in which patient safety is "owned" by all

The STEEEP® Quality Journey

Achieving health care that is safe, timely, effective, efficient, equitable and patient centered (STEEEP) is not an endpoint, but a journey. This journey requires a commitment to quality improvement (QI) from the highest levels of leadership combined with the interdependent development of several key components of health care delivery: administration and governance, clinical leadership, program development, data analytics, and accreditation. As each organization travels along its journey, these components must evolve at a common pace. With each component of a given phase of the quality journey firmly developed, the organization can expect to advance to the next phase knowing that the requisite factors are aligned.

Baylor Scott & White Health (BSWH) has traveled this journey during its 100 years as a quality leader. We see it as part of our mission to work with others to help them achieve the highest levels of quality and safety for their patients. Contact the BSWH STEEEP Global Institute today to find out how we can help your organization accelerate its STEEEP Quality Journey.

	INITIATION	FOUNDATION BUILDING	OPERATIONALIZING	CONTINUOUS QI
Administration and Governance	• Often unaware of potential benefits of QI • Often do not view QI as their responsibility and instead delegate to clinicians	• Understand the necessity of becoming involved in and providing leadership in QI • Become engaged in QI initiatives	• Directly involved in driving the organization to a culture of QI • Actively measure and reward improvement	• Fully engaged in, and see themselves as accountable for driving QI • Quality is an integral part of their, and the organization's incentive program
Physician and Nurse Leadership	• Often have marginal involvement in QI initiatives • Focus is primarily on clinical delivery and organizational issues	• Active engagement in some QI initiatives • Represent the clinicians and the patient in QI discussions and decisions	• Work together to identify and lead QI initiatives • Become the voice of the patient as well as the clinician	• Fully engaged in QI and drive innovation within their disciplines • Often responsible for engaging their professional communities in QI efforts
Quality Improvement Programs and Expertise	• Limited QI knowledge • Few formally established QI measurement tools and methodologies • Limited or basic safety programs in place	• Pockets of QI expertise • Formal QI structure in place with limited measureable impact • Quality and safety programs across some disciplines and/or facilities • Some best practice initiatives	• Deeper expertise shared across disciplines and/or facilities • Formal structure in place with moderate QI • Organization-wide quality and safety programs	• Established governance and infrastructure for managing and coordinating QI • Formalized QI training for staff at multiple levels • Fully integrated processes, practices, data and analysis • Decision support drives innovation
Data and Analytics	• Little or no ability to extract relevant data and report on quality measures • Data integrity often an issue and a point of debate	• Outcomes/quality measurement and reporting in some areas • Infrastructure capable of extracting data, but with little or no analysis or potential for organizational impact • Quality of data improving and slowly becoming accepted in a number of areas of the organization	• Ability to extract and analyze data to drive QI initiatives • Data integrity no longer an issue and accepted in most areas of the organization	• Established procedures and timelines for data collection and analysis • Development and implementation of data-driven, clinical and operational best practices • Data is used to drive the incentive system for the organization
Reputation/Accreditation	• Basic/minimal accreditation	• Local reputation • Some advanced accreditation	• Regional reputation • Advanced accreditation in several areas	• Nationally recognized as a leader in quality, safety and innovation

STEEEP®

BaylorScott&White HEALTH

Figure I.2 The STEEEP Quality Journey.

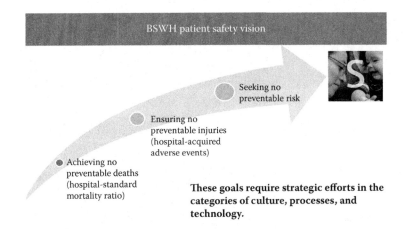

Figure I.3   Progressive vision for safe care.

facilities, departments, and employees. Processes for improving patient safety should align with national priorities as well as existing and planned organizational programs and should be associated with specific outcomes that can be measured and reported. In the area of technology, health information technology (HIT) and electronic health records (EHRs) can improve patient safety, but their complexity can lead to unintended consequences, which is one reason the study of human factors is critical to the development and implementation of an organizational patient safety program. This book will describe the patient safety journey as it progresses through the stages of building the foundation, creating the culture, integrating the culture, building the processes, and leveraging technology.

Chapter 1

Building the Foundation

Transforming the culture, processes, and technology of an organization to align with the priorities of a new patient safety program is both challenging and exciting and requires a broad foundation (see Figure 1.1). The journey to safe patient care begins with an explicit governance commitment to patient safety; the establishment of organization, department, and employee goals that reflect this commitment; the implementation of patient safety training programs for new and existing employees; and changes to the infrastructure of the organization, including the addition of key departments, roles, and committees dedicated to improving patient safety.

Governance

To instill an organizational culture in which all employees—regardless of whether they are involved in direct patient care—prioritize patient safety, leaders at the highest levels need to make a formal commitment to the patient safety journey and communicate this commitment throughout the organization. BSWH board leaders have affirmed their commitment to patient safety with several formal resolutions. The first resolution, which was passed in 2000 and reaffirmed in 2010, reads:

> Whereas, maintaining the status quo or achieving quality and safety levels only equal to or slightly better than national, regional, or local norms is not compatible with the organization's Vision and Mission Statements; and

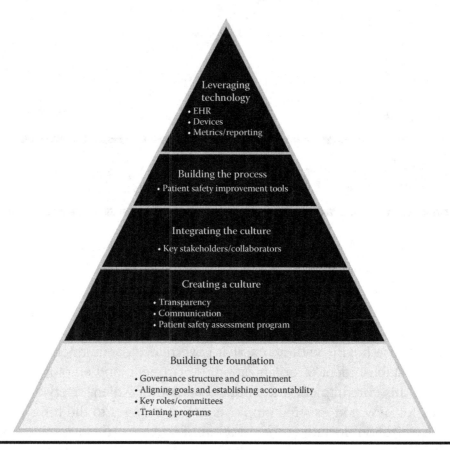

Figure 1.1   Patient safety framework for achieving safe health care. EHR, Electronic health record.

Whereas, regulatory and legislative changes and a growing number of more informed patients support better quality patient care and safety;

Therefore, be it resolved, that the Board of Trustees of Baylor Health Care System hereby challenges itself and everyone involved in providing health care throughout the system to give patient safety and continuous improvement in the quality of patient care the highest priority in the planning, budgeting, and execution of all activities in order to achieve significant, demonstrable, and measurable positive improvement in the quality of patient care and safety.

This resolution established the organization's strong commitment to safety and quality and empowered leaders and employees throughout the system to plan, budget, and execute activities based on this ongoing commitment.

The Board of Trustees resolved to take more specific action to improve patient safety in 2005, after the Institute for Healthcare Improvement (IHI) launched its "100,000 Lives Campaign" to save 100,000 lives over 18 months through six patient safety interventions:

- Deploy rapid response teams (RRTs) at the first sign of patient decline
- Deliver reliable, evidence-based care for acute myocardial infarction (AMI) to prevent deaths from heart attack
- Prevent adverse drug events by implementing medication reconciliation
- Prevent central line infections by implementing a series of interdependent, scientifically grounded steps called the Central Line Bundle
- Prevent surgical site infections by reliably delivering the correct perioperative antibiotics at the proper time
- Prevent ventilator-associated pneumonia by implementing a series of interdependent, scientifically grounded steps including the Ventilator Bundle (Berwick et al. 2006)

Recognizing the importance of the 100,000 Lives Campaign to patient safety as well as the need to align organizational priorities with national priorities, a board resolution was passed in 2005 committing the organization to "rapidly implement" these six programs and established a target of reducing the inpatient mortality rate by at least 4% from fiscal year 2005 to fiscal year 2006, both at the individual hospital level and in aggregate across the system. The resolution expanded the focus of patient safety from prevention of in-hospital deaths to preventing incidents of medical harm, reflecting a more proactive approach to safety.

Soon after the above board resolution was adopted, a nurse on the medical/surgical floor of a BSWH facility assessed her patient and felt that something was wrong. The patient's vital signs and laboratory tests suggested that the patient was stable. But the nurse, knowing her patient, sensed that something was wrong even though she couldn't determine exactly what it was. She called the physician. The physician reviewed the patient's charts and also found that the patient's assessment, including vital signs and laboratory tests, was normal. The physician told the nurse to continue to monitor the patient and let him know immediately if there were any changes in the patient's condition. After hanging up the phone,

despite no change in the patient's clinical picture, the nurse con-
tinued to have that "gut feeling" that something was wrong, so she
called the RRT. The RRT arrived and, after performing a thorough
assessment, determined that the patient was showing very early
signs of sepsis. The patient was transferred to the intensive care unit
and treated for sepsis. This patient made a full and rapid recovery.

Goals and Accountability

After an organizational commitment to patient safety has been established at
the highest levels of leadership, the organization and all its employees need
to understand their accountability for patient safety and establish formal
goals that reflect this commitment. BSWH sets annual system-wide goals
across four areas of focus:

■ Quality: Deliver STEEEP care, supported by education and research.
■ People: Be the best place to work.
■ Service: Serve both our patients and our community.
■ Finance: Be responsible financial stewards.

These goals cascade to employees at all levels of the organization, and
a performance award program places a portion of executive pay "at risk"
depending on the extent to which the goals are achieved (Ballard 2003;
Ballard et al. 2014; Herrin et al. 2008). Aligning incentives with goals has
allowed BSWH to adopt STEEEP aims throughout the organization and hold
leaders and employees accountable for specific actions that drive patient
safety. For example, BSWH's fiscal year 2015 goals related to patient safety
(in the quality area of focus) include the following:

■ Improved performance across clinical processes of care for AMI,
community-acquired pneumonia (PNE), surgical infection prevention,
and influenza immunization
■ Reduction in 30-day hospital readmission rates for patients with AMI,
chronic obstructive pulmonary disease, heart failure, PNE, total hip
arthroplasty, and total knee arthroplasty
■ Reduction in hospital-acquired conditions (HACs), including catheter-
associated urinary tract infections (CAUTI), and central line-associated
bloodstream infections (CLABSI)

■ Improved performance across the patient safety indicators composite (PSI-90s), defined as the risk-adjusted ratio of observed to expected encounters that qualify for selected Agency for Healthcare Research and Quality (AHRQ) patient safety indicator measures for potentially preventable adverse events

All goals are SMART (specific, measureable, actionable, realistic, and time-bound), defining specific improvement levels and dates by which these improvements should be achieved. Progress toward achieving system-level goals is presented to the Board of Trustees and the Senior Leadership Council in the monthly STEEEP Care report, facilitating continuous analysis of data and trends and development of action plans to address opportunities for improvement.

These same goals are transmitted to the medical staff physician champions, both in patient safety and in quality, who lead clinical teams to improve and implement clinical processes across the system. Results are measured, tracked, and reported to the medical staff at Medical Executive Committees and other physician forums.

An example is the development of the HAC Reduction Program to improve performance around the BSWH fiscal year 2015 patient safety goal. The HAC Reduction Program Charter outlines the following purpose and scope of work:

Purpose:

The Hospital-Acquired Conditions Reduction Steering Committee will provide leadership oversight to improve specific conditions impacting quality and patient safety of BSWH patients. In addition, this work will help drive performance to a desirable level of improvement while avoiding financial penalty.

Scope of Work:

– Develop and support system HAC Reduction Subcommittees to implement a standard framework for all BSWH facilities
– Support the development of facility HAC Reduction teams to lead individual facility improvement efforts through teamwork and collaboration, while pursuing a culture of safety and accountability
– The designated facility leader (Patient Safety Officer, Health Care Improvement Director, or Central Division Quality representative) facilitates data collection and dissemination, improvement efforts, interventions, and work plans through multidisciplinary teams at facility/institution. Designated facility team leader will report up to the appropriate HAC Reduction subcommittee team

- Engage executive leadership, medical staff, Chief Medical Officer (CMO), Chief Nursing Officer (CNO), and Physician Patient Safety Champion in patient safety efforts
- Report selected process and outcome metrics monthly for applicable focus areas to appropriate HAC Reduction subcommittee and Steering Committee using the HAC/PSI-90 monthly summary
- Incorporate additional HAC indicators as they become part of Centers for Medicare and Medicaid Services (CMS) rules to be measured

The BSWH HAC Reduction Steering Committee scope of work and facility workflow for HACs are presented in Figure 1.2.

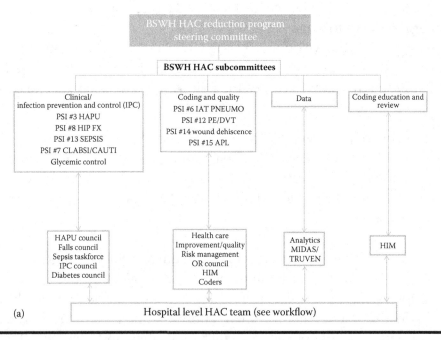

Figure 1.2 (a) HAC Reduction Steering Committee scope of work. APL, accidental puncture or laceration; BSWH, Baylor Scott & White Health; CAUTI, catheter-associated urinary tract infection; CLABSI, central line-associated bloodstream infection; HAC, hospital-acquired condition; HAPU, hospital-acquired pressure ulcer; HIM, health information management; IAT PNEUMO, iatrogenic pneumothorax; OR, operating room; PE/DVT, pulmonary embolism/deep vein thrombosis; PSI, patient safety indicator. *(Continued)*

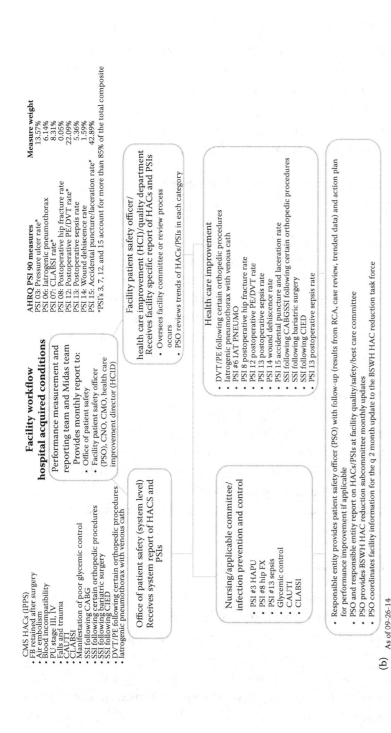

Figure 1.2 (Continued)   (b) HAC Reduction Steering Committee facility workflow. AHRQ, Agency for Healthcare Research and Quality; BSWH, Baylor Scott & White Health; CABG, coronary artery bypass graft; CAUTI, catheter-associated urinary tract infection; CIED, cardiac implantable electronic device; CLABSI, central line-associated bloodstream infection; CMO, chief medical officer; CMS, centers for medicare and medicaid services; CNO, chief nursing officer; DVT/PE, deep vein thrombosis/pulmonary embolism; FB, foreign body; FX, fracture; HAC, hospital-acquired condition; HAPU, hospital-acquired pressure ulcer; IAT PNEUMO, iatrogenic pneumothorax; IPPS, inpatient prospective payment system; PSI, patient safety indicator; PU, pressure ulcer; SSI, surgical site infection.

Training

In addition to the commitment to patient safety supported by formal goals that cascade to all employees, organizations should establish training programs that emphasize patient safety for both new and existing employees. Although the specific training programs will vary across organizations, some important examples include new employee orientation, process improvement training, clinician leadership training, and human factors training. These programs are described in more detail further in the chapter.

> *With training, employees establish the knowledge that safety is not a foreign concept but a science with principles they already understand and use every day. As a BSWH employee who specializes in patient safety measurement explains, "When I was a kid, we had one phone in the middle of the house. Mom had a rule that when she was dialing the phone, you couldn't interrupt her. In other words, she identified a high-risk time and asked not to be distracted. This is a lesson we can apply to patient care. When we order food, the server reads back the order and verifies. People are used to these practices. Every day, when you leave the house, you perform a mental checklist to make sure you remembered your keys, your wallet, and your briefcase. Patient safety is something that should be so ingrained in your actions that you would feel awkward if you didn't follow its principles. Seat belts are an example—we feel awkward if we don't wear our seat belts. Let employees know that these concepts are easy for them to understand and apply."*

New Employee Orientation

Creating and sustaining an organizational culture of patient safety requires that new employees are introduced to the patient safety program as soon as they are hired. At BSWH, all new employees participate in a system-wide orientation and new employees who will be associated with a specific facility also undergo a facility orientation. Patient safety is an important element of both types of orientation. In the system-wide orientation, new employees are introduced to the Stop the Line policy (Graban 2009), a crucial element of the organization's patient safety program.

The purpose of the Stop the Line policy is to encourage and support any employee, staff member, contract staff member, student, volunteer, vendor, patient, family member, or visitor to intervene when a patient safety risk is believed to exist. Anyone can stop the line by using direct communication with a caregiver who is engaged in or is about to engage in an action believed to be an unintentional risk to patient safety. The policy encourages the use of critical language to confirm or restore patient safety. "Critical language" means that specific words are used to convey the need to stop and evaluate patient safety. An example of critical language is the phrase "I need some clarity."

The Stop the Line policy has the following goals:

■ To support every person who speaks up to protect patient safety
■ To communicate that all caregivers are expected to respond to a Stop the Line request
■ To emphasize that it is unacceptable for anyone to ignore a Stop the Line attempt or retaliate against someone who stops the line in good faith

An important component of The Stop the Line policy is educating all staff to recognize and respond to the critical language. This is accomplished by a comprehensive implementation plan inclusive of all hospital staff.

While the Stop the Line policy is a crucial part of the BSWH patient safety program, its purpose is to support a culture in which all members of the organization feel comfortable "speaking up" for patient safety.

The Stop the Line flowchart used at BSWH is depicted in Figure 1.3.

A technologist was preparing a patient for radiology testing when he began to question whether the test was appropriate based on the patient's medical history. Using National Patient Safety Goal 1–Improve the Accuracy of Patient Identification (using name and date of birth)—the employee compared the patient's name and date of birth to the order received. He used Stop the Line to seek clarification and discovered that the radiology test had been ordered for a different patient. "This employee's due diligence and commitment to patient safety prevented an error from occurring," says the hospital's clinical risk manager and patient safety officer.

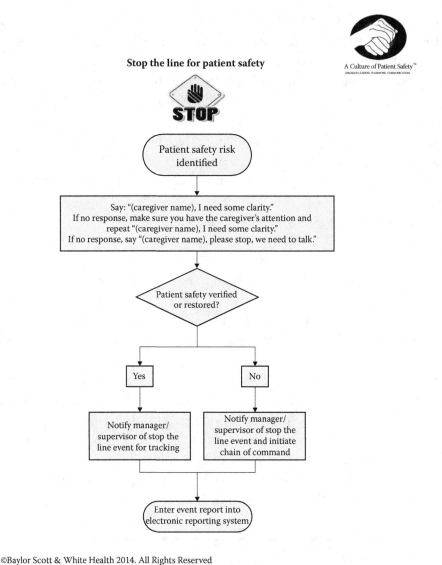

Figure 1.3   **Stop the line flowchart.**

In addition to the system-wide new employee orientation that introduces the Stop the Line policy, orientations for new BSWH employees exist at the facility level. Although these are more diverse because of the different characteristics of the individual facilities, they have common themes that include the need for all employees to "own" patient safety. For example, across several BSWH facilities, newly hired nurse managers participate in "Nurse Manager Boot Camp," an orientation program that introduces participants to the organizational culture of patient safety and teaches skills for improving

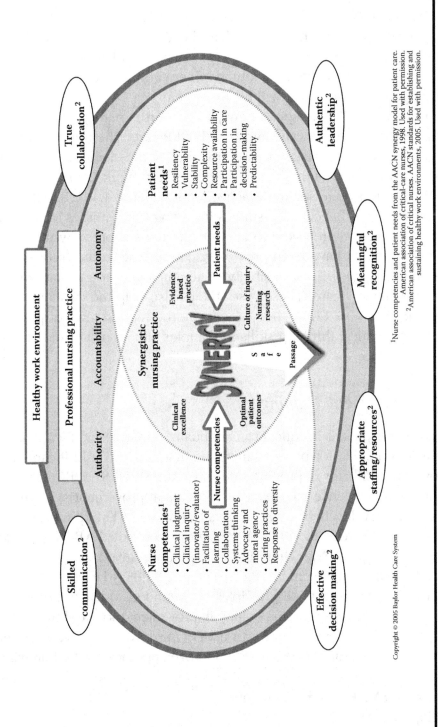

[1]Nurse competencies and patient needs from the AACN synergy model for patient care. American association of critical-care nurses, 1998. Used with permission. [2]American association of critical nurses. AACN standards for establishing and sustaining healthy work environments, 2005. Used with permission.

Figure 1.4   BSWH professional nursing practice model.

patient safety. Nurse Manager Boot Camp is one day a week for four weeks and is held ten times per year. Newly hired nurse leaders, learn about the BSWH Professional Nursing Practice Model (Figure 1.4), including its six elements of effective decision making, shared collaboration, authentic leadership, meaningful recognition, skilled communication, and appropriate staffing. These six factors promote a healthy work environment and drive safe patient passage throughout the health care system.

At a small, rural BSWH hospital, newly hired nurses participate in a facility orientation that introduces the aims of STEEEP care. The nurses then form small groups and are asked to identify and list the elements of a great health care environment as they relate to the Healthy Work Environment of the BSWH Professional Nursing Practice Model (Figure 1.4). They then examine several hypothetical case studies involving "near misses" that could impact patient care and are asked to answer questions about how the hypothetical situation could have been prevented. These case studies provide examples emphasizing the responsibility of all employees to facilitate the delivery of safe patient care. These case studies also help the new nurses to think proactively about how they can ensure the highest level of patient safety and apply critical thinking skills in complex situations to guide their own nursing practice.

Process Improvement Training

For existing employees, it is critical to continually reinforce the idea that everyone is accountable for patient safety, the first aim of STEEEP care, and to teach ongoing skills for improving safe care. At BSWH, STEEEP Academy and Operational Excellence courses teach process improvement skills and help students to develop their own projects to improve STEEEP care.

In 2004, BHCS founded the STEEEP Academy (then called ABC Baylor) to teach physicians, nurses, other clinicians, and administrative leaders methods of rapid-cycle quality improvement (Ballard et al. 2014; Haydar et al. 2009). Course participants learn general principles of continuous quality improvement as well as health care-specific quality improvement tools and finish the course by designing and implementing a quality improvement project. Course topics as they relate to rapid-cycle quality improvement include the following:

■ Creation of SMART Aim Statements
■ Development of a team

- Process Modeling
- Identification of Metrics
- Prioritization of Improvement Targets
- Implementation and Data Collection
- Data Analysis
- Sustainability and Spread

The Operational Excellence Program (then called Lean Academy) was founded at SWH in 2009. From their inception, Operational Excellence programs have been designed to meet the needs of their specific audiences. Several types of courses are offered:

- Two-hour courses designed to enable staff to attend training modules
- Operational Excellence Fundamentals course for all new employees
- Four-day advanced Operational Excellence training that any employee can attend
- Lean Management Systems training for leaders

These courses teach the daily practices of continually searching out waste in daily work and the importance of involving staff in daily problem identification and problem solving. Leaders are responsible for building Visual Control Metric tracking boards called huddle boards to track performance and involve staff in continuous problem solving as a part of their responsibilities.

In addition, continuing education credits can be earned through certain Operational Excellence courses and STEEEP Academy.

Like STEEEP Academy, Operational Excellence courses teach the plan–do–check–act model of rapid-cycle quality improvement. These programs support the elements of STEEEP care by emphasizing the need to do what's right for the patient while eliminating waste and improving efficiency. Overall, STEEEP Academy and Operational Excellence courses promote a culture of continuous improvement focused on STEEEP care (Figure 1.5).

Leadership Training

Physician leadership and nurse leadership are crucial to the ability of health care organizations to create and maintain a culture of patient safety.

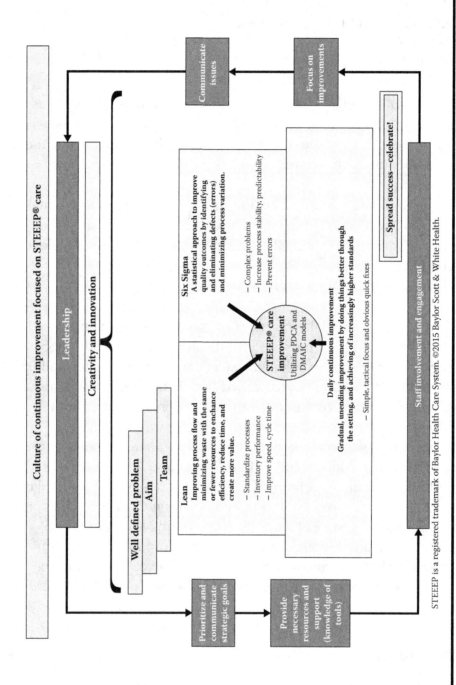

Figure 1.5 Culture of continuous improvement focused on STEEEP care. DMAIC, Define, Measure, Analyze, Improve, and Control; PDCA, Plan, Do, Check, Act.

Physician and nurse leaders have a powerful role as champions for patient safety processes and evolving technology that drive safe care. For physician leaders, BSWH offers an introductory physician leadership course and an advanced physician leadership development course. The one-day introductory leadership course is offered each year to approximately seventy physicians who are selected by organizational leaders. The course facilitates enhanced collaboration among physicians and supports the role of physician leaders in improving STEEEP care (Convery et al. 2012). The advanced course, which is offered by BSWH and the Southern Methodist University (SMU) Cox School of Business, includes six full-day sessions spread out over two years. Fifty physician leaders participate in these courses (Ballard et al. 2014; Convery et al. 2012).

For nurse leaders, BSWH offers the Advancing Nursing Excellence Scholarship Program to encourage nurses to pursue advanced academic degrees, as well as the Nurse Executive Fellowship Program with the SMU Cox School of Business. The latter program prepares twenty-five nurse leaders each year for progressive leadership roles by providing twelve intensive workshops and concluding with the design and completion of a capstone project that demonstrates patient care improvement as well as a financial return on investment. In addition, BSWH offers the Achieving Synergy in Practice through Impact, Relationships, and Evidence (ASPIRE) program to promote growth in practice, education, research, and leadership by encouraging nurses to undertake quality improvement projects, research studies, and community outreach initiatives. The goals of the ASPIRE program are to:

■ Empower nurses to recognize and communicate the difference they make for patient outcomes
■ Differentiate professional nursing practice in terms of accountability, autonomy, and authority as it relates to outcomes
■ Promote collegiality, mentoring, and leadership in nursing
■ Foster the development of new knowledge, skills, and attitudes
■ Embrace innovation and evidence-based decision making (Ballard et al. 2014)

By emphasizing accountability for patient outcomes as well as evidence-based decision making, these goals align with the aims of STEEEP care and help to promote patient safety.

Human Factors Training

> *Connectors that are used with medical equipment or to deliver fluids or gases can be inadvertently connected with other medical devices. Serious patient harm, including death, can occur if fluids, medications, or nutrition formulas are administered via the incorrect route. A new type of connector has recently been designed by an International Organization of Standardization (ISO) standards development process. Standards for this newly designed connector make it difficult, if not impossible, for unrelated delivery systems to be connected, thereby facilitating an error-proof connection process (Guenter 2014).*

Human factors include all the factors that influence people and their behavior, from environmental factors to organizational factors to individual personality characteristics. In a health care setting, some common areas that human factors influence related to patient safety include:

- Mental workload
- Distractions
- Physical environment and workflow
- Physical demands
- Device/product design
- Teamwork
- Process design

Increased awareness and training in this area can drive safe patient care by fostering an understanding of how errors in health care are made, improving the safety culture of teams and organizations, enhancing teamwork and communication, improving the design of health care systems and equipment, and enhancing the ability of health care teams to predict and prevent errors (Carthey and Clarke).

The Human Factors group at BSWH has developed training modules for employees to introduce them to human factors, how these factors can impact patient safety, and how they can be improved to drive safer patient care. The table of contents for the "Human Factors 101" workshop is displayed in Figure 1.6.

Human Factors "101"
What Every Healthcare Professional Needs to Know

Introduction to human factors
- What is human factors?
- Concepts: What are "use errors"
- Case: Defibrillators unintentionally powered off
- Case: Heparin 1000 fold dosing error

Observe how work is done
- Concept: Observe, not assume, how work is done
- Methods: How to observe
- Case: Sterilized racks in sterile processing unit

Make reading easier and safer
- Concept: Human reading
- Methods: Simplifying and grouping in displays
- Cases: Hemodialysis heparin, Penicillamine? Penicillin?, diet order electronic health record screen design, radiology acquisition form design, and crash cart redesign

Consider limits in memory
- Concepts: Short-term memory, omission, and confirmation bias
- Case: Collapsing operating table and infusion pump programming errors

Error proofing
- Concept: Forcing function
- Method: When and how to use forcing function
- Case: Automatic blood pressure cuff misconnection
- Everyday examples of forcing function

Improve the worksystem
- Concept: Health care as a worksystem
- Case: Patient identification for operating room specimen

Reduce interruptions & distractions
- Concept: Interruptions and distractions lead to increased errors and decrease efficiency
- Concept: Common sources of interruptions

Improve teamwork & communication
- Concepts: Common barriers in teamwork and in speaking up, and differences in perspectives
- Case: New nurse calling physician at night

Additional Resources
- Additional reading materials
- Additional examples of visual designs
- Additional case studies of human factors improvement
- Toolkit for improving nursing worksystem
- Additional concepts for teamwork and communication
- Human factors and electronic health record

Human Factors @ Baylor Scott & White Health © 2014

Figure 1.6 Table of contents for Human Factors 101 Workshop.

Infrastructure

Once the organizational foundation has been established with strong governance, challenging but achievable goals, and accountability for patient safety by all members across the organization, and patient safety training is in place, the next critical step is strong infrastructure support to sustain and promote patient safety. First, the governance commitment to patient safety described earlier in this chapter will inform the patient safety strategy for the entire organization. After that commitment is in place, the organization should establish a department dedicated to patient safety, define key patient safety roles and committees, and create a data and analytics department to measure patient safety improvements.

Office of Patient Safety

For an organization to develop, implement, and measure the impact of patient safety initiatives, formal infrastructure and resources should be dedicated to the creation of a comprehensive, organization-wide patient safety department. This group will lead the adoption of patient safety culture, processes, and technology throughout the organization and will determine initiatives to address opportunities for improvement identified by analysis and measurement (Ballard 2015).

In 2005, BSWH established the Office of Patient Safety, which has achieved significant standardization of safety processes and implementation of evidence-based patient safety practices. The Office of Patient Safety seeks to strengthen existing patient safety programs, promote an organizational culture conducive to recognizing and resolving situations that pose a risk of patient injury, develop patient safety innovations, and guide employees in the adoption of the values of a patient safety culture (Kennerly et al. 2011). The Office of Patient Safety created 12 Guiding Principles of Safe Design and Operations:

1. Minimize fatigue and distraction that interfere with effectiveness.
2. Improve patient "handoffs" to prevent errors when patients move to, from, and within the organization.
3. Make verbal and written communication more effective to improve teamwork.
4. With any high-risk care process, involve two people to avoid error.
5. Pay attention to alerts, alarms, and warning that can prevent patient harm.
6. Take ownership. "Fix what you can; tell what you fixed; if you can't fix it, find someone who can."
7. Standardize and simplify processes to prevent errors.
8. Don't assume someone else will do what is needed. Clarify roles and responsibilities to prevent gaps in care.
9. Use evidence-based staffing.
10. Involve patients/families as partners in achieving safe care.
11. Provide rapid access to user-friendly clinical data and decision support tools.
12. Provide a physical work environment that supports safe care.

Key Roles and Committees

In a multihospital health care system, each facility should have a patient safety officer or person designated to oversee patient safety initiatives. It is key to have at least one patient safety physician champion with dedicated hours to focus on patient safety. At BSWH, these leaders interface with the system-wide Office of Patient Safety and ensure that organizational best practices for patient safety are spread throughout each facility and department. In addition, the BSWH Office of Patient Safety relies on the system-level Patient Safety Committee, which has broad professional and institutional representation, to advise and guide its activities and initiatives. The charter of the Patient Safety Committee states that its purpose is to "provide a formal administrative environment to assess, monitor and mitigate risks to patient safety and outcomes in all areas of the organization that result in deaths or injuries that might be avoided." The primary role of the Patient Safety Committee is to provide direction to leaders, staff, and other resources of the Office of Patient Safety, as well as to influence the work of other STEEEP committees, service lines, and departments through collaboration. The Patient Safety Committee is chaired by the chief patient safety officer, and committee members include both clinicians and leaders with expertise or interest in patient safety.

In addition to the Patient Safety Committee, examples of other committees important to patient safety include the following:

■ The Clinical Data Access Team (CDAT) functions as a high-level work group and exists to ensure access to information needed for patient care. The CDAT also measures and reports information systems data such as preventive maintenance, time required for a service request, and planned and unplanned downtimes and system availability. The Charter was updated in 2015 and is composed of multidisciplinary physician, operational, technical, and clinician representatives.

■ HIT functions with delegated authority from the BSWH Patient Safety Committee to provide an administrative environment to assess and mitigate risks related to the safety of patient care associated with various aspects of HIT. A formal Charter was approved in late 2011 and is composed of physician, clinician, and technical representatives.

■ The Device Safety Subcommittee focuses on medical devices with clinical users. A formal charter was approved in 2012. This group supports infusion pump safety, alarm management, ongoing review of technology hazards, and support of recall actions as well as other device-related projects and initiatives (see Figure 1.7).

The BSWH patient safety committee and subcommittee structure is presented in Figure 1.8.

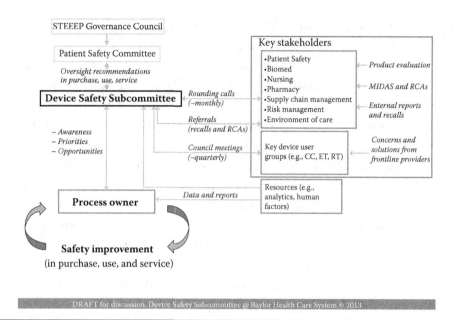

Figure 1.7 Device safety improvement framework. CC, Critical Care; ET, Emergency Therapist; RCA, Root Cause Analysis; RT, Respiratory Therapist.

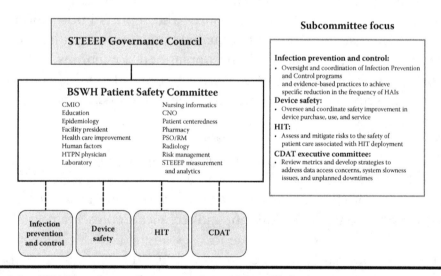

Figure 1.8 BSWH patient safety structure. CDAT, Clinical Data Access Team; CMIO, Chief Medical Information Officer; CNO, Chief Nursing Officer; HAIs, Hospital Associated Infections; HIT, Health information technology; HTPN, HealthTexas Provider Network; PSO/RM, Patient Safety Officer/Risk Manager; STEEEP, Safe, Timely, Effective, Efficient, Equitable, and Patient-Centered.

Data and Analytics

The establishment of a data and analytics department is essential for measuring and reporting the impact of patient safety initiatives. This department includes statisticians, database analysts, and programmers with the ability to develop capabilities to organize, use, and report the organization's patient safety data, including the following:

■ Database development and management through advanced programming
■ Resources to support the reporting of patient safety indicators
■ Integration of data from multiple sources within the organization as well as state, regional, and national databases for benchmarking purposes (e.g., CMS, The Joint Commission)
■ Management of data from EHRs
■ Resources to support organization-wide standardized reporting and data requests (Ballard 2015; Ballard et al. 2014)

Smaller health care organizations or single hospitals may need to scale this work to their size and needs. They will need to determine the metrics and their success or improvement opportunities by collecting, analyzing, and reporting data to both the administrative and the clinical staff, as well as to the board. This is essential to measure progress along the journey.

Conclusion

An organizational commitment to patient safety that influences culture, processes, and technology requires a strong foundation. The journey to safer patient care begins with a commitment to patient safety from the highest levels of organizational leadership; the commitment and engagement of all staff across the organization; the development of organizational patient safety goals that are cascaded to all employees; the implementation of training programs that emphasize patient safety; and the addition of key departments and committees dedicated to improving patient safety and supported by a robust data and analytics resource. Once these elements are in place, the organization will be well positioned to progress to the second phase of its journey, which involves the creation of a culture of patient safety.

Chapter 2

Creating a Culture

Once the foundation of a patient safety program has been established, the next step in the journey toward safer patient care is for the organization to create a culture in which all leaders, employees, and physicians drive patient safety aims, plans, and initiatives. A culture of patient safety is characterized by the ability of everyone to feel comfortable and supported in speaking up; recognition of staff who "speak up" to prevent errors or enhance safety; communication of questions, concerns, and ideas through Patient Safety WalkRounds™ and TalkRounds; Patient Safety Officer Huddle Calls; and the use of an organizational patient safety culture survey with site visits to understand and communicate about areas of strength and opportunities for improvement. Patient safety should not represent additional work to the staff but should be part of their daily routine (see Figure 2.1).

Transparency

A culture of patient safety is based on transparency. As described in Chapter 1, BSWH sets annual organization-wide goals across four areas of focus: quality, service, people, and finance. Safer patient care is the aim of several of these goals, including improved performance across clinical processes of care for patients with certain illnesses or conditions, reduction of 30-day hospital readmission rates, reduction of HACs including CAUTI and CLABSI, and improved performance for potentially preventable adverse events. Progress toward achieving the system-level goals is presented to the Board of Trustees and the Senior Leadership Council in the monthly STEEEP Best

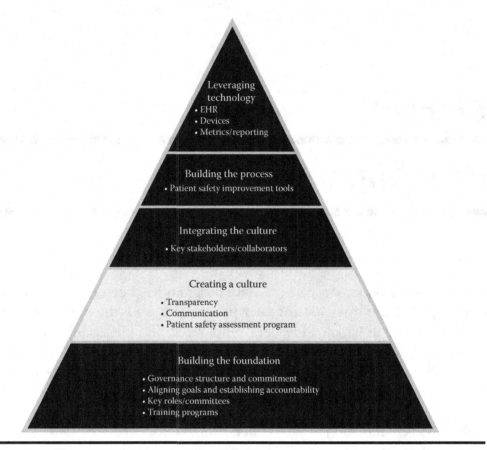

Figure 2.1 Patient safety framework for achieving safe health care. EHR, Electronic health record.

Care Report, which displays performance across each goal area at the system and facility levels. This report is also shared with the medical staff at regular meetings. The STEEEP Best Care Report is also shared on the organization's intranet website so that all employees can view the organization's current goals and its ongoing progress toward achieving them (Ballard et al. 2014).

In addition to the STEEEP Best Care Report, the organization-wide patient safety dashboard provides an overview of each facility's performance across a variety of patient safety measures, including the following:

- National Patient Safety Goal 01.01.01: Patient Identification
- National Patient Safety Goal 02.03.01: Critical Test Result Reporting (for laboratory tests)
- National Patient Safety Goal 02.03.01: Critical 12-Lead EKG Results
- National Patient Safety Goal 03.04.01: Medication Labeling on and off the Sterile Field

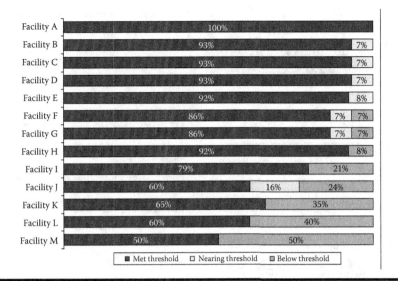

Figure 2.2 **Hospital attainment of sample patient safety compliance goal: February 2015.**

- National Patient Safety Goal 07.01.01: Hand Hygiene
- National Patient Safety Goal 15.01.01: Suicide Risk
- Use of Universal Protocol in Non-Operating Room Areas
- Use of Universal Protocol in Operating Room Areas
- Percent of Staff Educated on Stop the Line
- Percent of Staff Educated on Situation, Background, Assessment, Recommendation (SBAR) Communication (see Chapter 4 for more information)
- Compliance with Infusion Pump libraries and safety features

Together, the STEEEP Best Care Report and the patient safety dashboard provide a clear and robust picture of how the organization and each of its facilities are performing across a variety of patient safety goals and indicators. An example of the patient safety dashboard is presented in Figure 2.2.

National Patient Safety Goals

As part of its commitment to aligning the BSWH patient safety program with national patient safety priorities, BSWH measures its performance across the Joint Commission National Patient Safety Goals (The Joint Commission, *National Patient Safety Goals*) and reports this performance in the patient

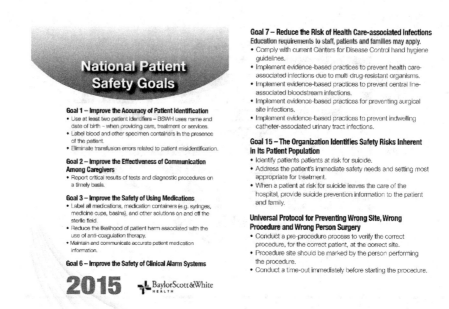

Figure 2.3 Badge tags displaying national patient safety goals.

safety dashboard. BSWH uses posters, flyers, and presentations to promote and publicize the National Patient Safety Goals. In addition, BSWH employees can wear tags on their security badges that display the National Patient Safety Goals (Figure 2.3).

Recognition of Staff

Responsibility for patient safety lies with every organizational member; therefore, it is crucial to recognize and reward employees when they "speak up" to prevent a patient safety risk or improve patient outcomes. An example of this type of recognition is the Good/Great Catch Program (facility specific), which recognizes employees who make a "Good/Great Catch" that prevents patient harm or enhances patient safety. Good/Great Catches occur when someone spots an error, problem, or safety risk before it reaches or impacts the patient. Examples of Good/Great Catches could include the omission of a patient armband; the mislabeling of a blood sample or other specimen; or incorrect medication order entry, dosing, or administration.

The goal of a patient safety recognition program is to create a fair and consistent culture where employees are empowered to identify patient safety opportunities. The recognized program is related to the Stop the Line policy, which supports and encourages staff and others to intervene when an imminent patient safety risk is believed to exist. Like the Stop the Line policy, the patient safety recognition program emphasizes that the organization values and encourages employees' efforts to improve patient safety and that it is unacceptable to retaliate or take disciplinary action against someone who speaks up for patient safety.

An employee who notices a patient safety event or occurrence and speaks up is asked to promptly alert his or her supervisor and enter the event into the organization's online reporting tool, which is accessible from the employee intranet portal. Employees may have the option of using a patient safety hotline to share patient safety events or occurrences. The hotline is an adjunct to the online reporting tool. If an employee calls the hotline and leaves a message, the person who listens to the message and follows up will enter the incident into the online reporting tool on the employee's behalf. In addition, if an employee overhears colleagues discussing an incident in which they stopped the line or identified a potential safety issue risk, the employee is asked to encourage these colleagues to report the incident to the organization's online reporting tool or the patient safety hotline.

Because feedback is critical in developing a culture of patient safety, recognition is provided in a variety of ways, including with certificates, leadership thank you notes, and employee newsletters. One BSWH facility recognizes Good Catches with the biannual "Fab 50" ceremony, which honors the employees responsible for the top fifty Good Catches. The ceremony is attended by the hospital president and chief executive officer, the hospital patient safety officer, the hospital patient safety manager, and a guest speaker who discusses a particular aspect of patient safety. Employees who are recognized at the ceremony receive Fab 50 jackets and are photographed for BSWH publications and posters.

In addition to recognizing and rewarding employees for speaking up, organizations should "close the loop" by using these data to drive improvements in safe care. At one BSWH facility, data from Great Catches are divided into categories (e.g., storage, facility design, prescription orders, medication dispensing) and action plans are developed to facilitate improvements across the top three reported types of Great Catches.

The success of any patient safety recognition program depends on the promotion of a culture in which employees are accountable for patient safety. Figure 2.4 describes the elements of this accountable culture: event reporting, speaking up for patient safety, responsibility for actions, environment, and trust among peers.

Accountability vs. Punitive Culture Survey

Safety and Risk Management

Patient Safety Indicator	Accountable Culture	Punitive Culture
Event Reporting	☐ Reporting is encouraged. ☐ Staff consider mistakes as evidence or clues of a faulty system.	☐ Reporting is discouraged ☐ Staff who report mistakes are punished
Speaking Up for Patient Safety	☐ Staff feel comfortable about speaking up for patient safety.	☐ Staff fear retaliation so they are hesitant and fearful to speak up for patient safety.
Responsibility for Actions	☐ Staff take personal responsibility for their actions and for the care that is rendered to patients.	☐ Staff blame others when errors occur.
Environment	☐ Staff feel comfortable about reporting and discussing events. ☐ "Lessons Learned" are shared with other teams to promote safety. ☐ Look first at the <u>process</u> when an error occurs.	☐ Staff feel uncomfortable about reporting and discussing events. ☐ Errors are not reported, therefore, there are no "Lessons" to be shared. ☐ Look first at the person when an error occurs.
Trust Among Peers	☐ Trust and mutual support are present throughout all levels of the organization. ☐ Managers follow HR guidelines regarding progressive corrective action.	☐ There is a lack of trust and mutual support between leaders and staff. ☐ Staff fear they are being "written up" by managers.

Figure 2.4 Accountable culture.

A senior technologist, while verifying the medical information for a heart transplant patient, discovered that the link to his medical history had been merged with that of another patient due to a computer glitch. Had the technologist not caught the error, another caregiver could have made a wrong decision based on the incorrect medical history. "The Fab 50 event was very memorable, and it meant a lot to me to be there," said the technologist. "But I was really just glad I was able to catch the error before it had an impact on patient care."

Three Words

Inspired by the ABC News Good Morning America "Your Three Words" segment, which asks viewers to submit videos describing their week in three words (ABC News), hospitals and health care systems have begun to encourage their employees to film videos in which they use three words to describe how they keep patients safe. Examples include "Keep Hallways Clear," "Read the Label," "Wash Your Hands," and "Protect Patient Privacy." One BSWH facility recently invited its departments to create and share their own "Three Words" videos. Participants from more than fifty departments submitted videos and were entered in a drawing for an airline ticket. A montage was created from the videos and shared on the employee intranet. HealthTexas Provider Network, the BSWH-affiliated multispecialty medical group, also launched a "Three Words" initiative.

Recognition programs like the Great Catch Program and the Fab 50 ceremony are necessary to creating a culture of patient safety. "These recognition programs are a good and easy way to get staff to understand that what they do makes a difference to patient safety and that leadership values them," says the patient safety manager at one BSWH facility. "The patient safety hotline is also easy and inexpensive to implement. It could even be done at a small hospital. This type of recognition leads to a culture where everyone feels safe speaking up. For example, a member of the housekeeping staff should feel comfortable stopping the line if a sharp is left on the sink, or if someone forgets to wash their hands." Spreading success stories helps to sustain patient safety initiatives, and recognizing employees for their commitment to safer patient care drives a culture in which everyone in the organization is accountable for patient safety.

Patient Safety WalkRounds and TalkRounds

Like transparency and employee recognition, communication and trust are critical to creating and sustaining a culture of patient safety. Patient Safety WalkRounds and TalkRounds help to foster communication, trust, and sharing of ideas among leaders and employees.

WalkRounds, which were originally developed by IHI, enable senior leaders to demonstrate their commitment to patient safety and learn about the opportunities for improvement in their organizations by making regular rounds to discuss safety with frontline staff. IHI provides the following tips for conducting these WalkRounds:

■ Receive a commitment from senior executives for an hour every week. WalkRounds may need to be rescheduled but never canceled.

■ Keep discussions focused on safety; don't dilute the safety message by trying to cover other topics.

■ Involve several senior executives in the organization, not just the chief executive officer.

■ Communicate with managers so they understand why senior executives are visiting their departments and provide support to these WalkRounds.

■ Make sure that senior executives follow up and provide feedback to staff about issues raised during the WalkRounds.

■ Institute regular safety briefings. Pass along issues raised in the briefings (with names of the contributing staff members withheld) to the executives to talk about on their WalkRounds.

■ Take a digital camera so PowerPoint presentations can be developed for staff and quality council meetings using examples from WalkRounds.

■ Before leaving the unit, ask executives to summarize the issues and ask staff to prioritize two to three items to be addressed (Institute for Healthcare Improvement, *Conduct Patient Safety Leadership WalkRounds*).

BSWH uses WalkRounds and TalkRounds to create a culture of patient safety. To begin a rounding meeting, the executive states the purpose of the meeting and explains that he or she wants to know what is going well with respect to patient safety as well as what the concerns are. Questions can include the following:

■ Which patient safety initiatives are frontline staff working on?

■ What patient safety-related concerns do they have?

■ Are there any patient safety issues that they have tried to solve?

■ What is the pebble in their shoe, or what keeps them up at night?

■ Is there anything they can think of that could potentially harm a patient? If so, have they tried to correct these issues?

■ What do they think would help to correct these issues or enhance patient safety? After the meeting, it is important for executives to follow up with staff and explain how their concerns are being addressed. WalkRounds and TalkRounds are important because they demonstrate to frontline staff that organizational leaders support them in their commitment to patient safety and their efforts to drive safe patient care.

A sample Patient Safety TalkRounds log is presented in Figure 2.5.

Date		Unit / Department Name Patient Safety TalkRounds	

Opportunity	Department / Individual Ownership	Resolution
Things Going Great!		

Figure 2.5   Patient safety TalkRounds log.

Patient Safety Officer Huddle Calls

Patient Safety Officer Huddle Calls are opportunities for patient safety leaders across a facility to share successes, concerns, and advice. At BSWH, these calls happen once a month about two weeks after the Patient Safety/ Risk Management meeting. Patient safety and risk management leaders give advice and receive input and share success stories and best practices. Concerns and follow-up are also shared. Like Patient Safety WalkRounds and TalkRounds, these calls facilitate strong organization-wide communication regarding patient safety issues and networking on resolution to concerns shared.

Patient Safety Culture Survey

One of the most important things an organization can do to create and sustain a culture of patient safety is to regularly survey employees about the culture of their facility, including strengths and opportunities for improvement. The 1999 IOM report *To Err Is Human* asserted that the health care industry can improve patient safety by learning from high-reliability industries in hazardous sectors that take a systematic approach to managing safety, including by using questionnaires to gather data regarding employees' perceptions of the safety culture (Kohn et al. 1999). In addition, The Joint Commission requires that accredited hospitals "create and maintain a culture of safety and quality throughout the hospital" and that to meet this standard

(Standard LD.03.01.01), "leaders regularly evaluate the culture of safety and quality using valid and reliable tools" (The Joint Commission 2009).

Initial Survey Development

At BSWH, the development of the patient safety culture survey, the Attitudes and Practices of Patient Safety Survey (APPSS), began in 2002. The organization's patient safety leaders aimed to design a questionnaire that would enable patient safety culture data to be collected and aggregated at the unit/department level in an actionable and meaningful way so that administrative and clinical leaders could apply these data to the development and prioritization of patient safety improvement initiatives.

Each APPSS deployment is the initial component of a two-year assessment program (Figure 2.6). The first version of the APPSS included domains that were derived from the safety science and patient safety literature. A draft item list was constructed and reviewed by quality and safety professionals and hospital employees who provide direct patient care. Revisions were made based on their feedback, and each item was assigned to a primary concept domain by a content expert panel. A frequency Likert scale ("always," "most of the time," "sometimes," "rarely," and "never") was used for as many items as possible. The APPSS was piloted at one BSWH facility in 2003 and subsequently was further revised. Currently, the survey questions are organized into four domains: leadership, reporting and feedback, resources, and teamwork. A sample of the 2013 APPSS is displayed in Figure 2.6.

Attitudes and Practices of Patient Safety Survey 2013

Thank you for taking the time to complete this survey. Your responses are very important and will be kept anonymous.

Please allow 10-15 minutes to complete all of the items of this survey. There is no option to "save and return". The survey is complete once you have selected the "Submit" button on the last screen. Please do not forward this link to anyone.

Please rate each statement with the response that best describes your experience in the past 6 months.
**Senior facility leaders include President, Vice Presidents, Chief Operating Officer, Chief Nursing Officer, Physician Leaders (Vice President of Medical Affairs and Patient Safety Physician Champion), Directors*

	Strongly Agree	Agree	Neutral	Disagree	Strongly Disagree	N/A
Senior facility leaders* promote patient safety.	○	○	○	○	○	○
Senior facility leaders* make rounds on my unit / department to discuss various topics, including patient safety concerns.	○	○	○	○	○	○
My work environment is safe and secure.	○	○	○	○	○	○
The "Stop the Line" policy makes me feel more confident about speaking up to protect the safety of the patient.	○	○	○	○	○	○
Recognizing and reporting errors and hazardous conditions is encouraged and valued.	○	○	○	○	○	○

Figure 2.6 Attitudes and Practices of Patient Safety Survey 2013.

Survey Deployment

Since the 2003 pilot administration, the APPSS has been implemented across BSWH facilities on a biennial basis. Employees with direct patient care responsibilities, from frontline providers to clinical leaders, receive the survey. Questions about the surgical checklist and processes have been added for operating room staff. Physicians and advanced practice professionals receive a separate, shorter version of the survey, and the Information Services department also conducts a patient safety survey of its employees (see Chapter 5).

A formal process was implemented in 2009 where six months before the next survey administration, a workgroup comprising representatives from the departments of patient safety, survey design, biostatistics, risk management, pharmacy, laboratory, radiology, informatics, and patient experience, as well as physician and nurse leaders, is convened to review item-level data, item performance, evolving patient safety concepts in the literature, and organizational needs and decide whether any survey item needs to be revised. Once the workgroup has reached consensus on a list of items, it is presented to the Patient Safety Committee and selected facility- and system-level leaders for approval. See Figure 2.7 for more detail on this assessment program.

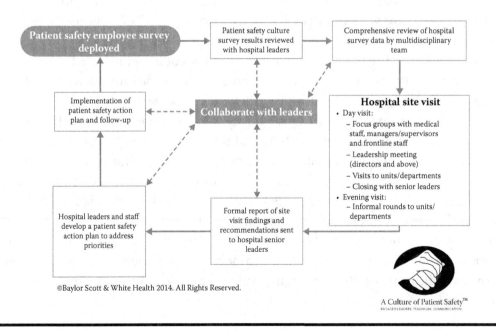

A Culture of Patient Safety™

Figure 2.7   Two-year cycle of patient safety assessment program.

The APPSS is deployed electronically. Employees with direct patient care responsibilities receive an e-mail inviting them to participate in the online survey; the e-mail includes a URL link to the survey. Employee data from the human resources databases are linked to the URL, eliminating the need for respondents to enter data related to their role, location, organizational longevity, and other relevant characteristics. To ensure anonymity, respondent identities are stripped from the data set during the data management process. The survey period lasts for three weeks, during which weekly reminders are sent to employees who have not yet submitted their response.

Survey Reports and Action Plans

Because the goal of the APPSS is to provide actionable data regarding the patient safety culture so these data can be used to guide improvement initiatives, BSWH has invested considerable effort in developing reports of survey results for organizational leaders. These reports provide domain-level and item-level data, using two main variables: (1) the percentage of respondents providing a "desirable response," defined as including the two most favorable responses ("strongly agree" and "agree," or "always" and "most of the time") and (2) the percentage of respondents providing a "highly desirable response" ("strongly agree" or "always"). This format allows leaders to identify areas of high performance and areas where improvement is needed.

In addition, a Priority Index is calculated for each facility to identify individual survey items that serve as recommendations for improvement initiatives and action plans. The priority index score for each question is found by first finding the improvement opportunity, which is the difference between the current performance of the item and a perfect score (100%). Second, the correlation between each item and the overall safety rating is found. This correlation shows the strength of the relationship between each item and the primary outcome question. Next, the priority index score is found by taking the improvement opportunity and multiplying that by the correlation to the overall safety rating. This produces a score that prioritizes items with poor performance (i.e., having more opportunity for improvement) and gives more weight to those items with a strong relationship to the primary outcome question.

For example, if item 1 has a 20% opportunity for improvement and item 2 has a 16% opportunity for improvement, and if the correlations to the overall safety rating are .50 and .75, respectively, for items 1 and 2, then the priority index scores would be 10 and 12. This would suggest that improvement on item 2 would result in a greater effect on the primary outcome question than would improvement on item 1. Potential high-priority items for patient safety are presented in Figure 2.8.

Survey finding/reports are transparent so that leaders from each hospital can compare their hospital's performance with other hospitals' performance and with the performance of the system as a whole. The reports also allow facility leaders to compare results among job categories and type of units/ departments within their facilities and to observe trends and changes in the data over time.

Potential High-Priority Items for PS

The items below are listed in order of their combined rank of being <u>both</u> important to staff's perception of PS <u>and</u> having greater opportunity for improvement.

1. Senior facility leaders make rounds on my unit / department to discuss various topics, including patient safety concerns
2. This facility deals effectively with poor performance among the following staff – Doctors
3. This facility deals effectively with poor performance among the following staff – Managers
4. This facility deals effectively with disruptive behavior among the following staff – Doctors
5. I have seen positive changes in practice as a result of reporting errors and near misses
6. In my unit / department people treat each other with respect
7. On my unit / department the staffing is adequate to provide safe, consistent care
8. This facility deals effectively with disruptive behavior among the following staff – Managers
9. I do not worry about being punished when I report errors or near misses
10. I have what I need to deliver safe care

Figure 2.8 Potential high-priority items for patient safety.

Patient Safety Site Visits

> *One early discovery from the APPSS and patient safety site visits was that frontline employee staff wanted an official Stop the Line policy. They wanted an organization-wide policy so they would be protected if they spoke up and stopped the line. BSWH leaders developed and implemented the Stop the Line policy (see Chapter 1), but they understood that Stop the Line was really about the organizational patient safety culture—about ensuring that leaders were supportive of Stop the Line, and that everyone knew the critical language ("I need some clarity") of stopping the line. Since then, education on Stop the Line has expanded significantly. New employees are introduced to the policy and process in orientation, and the patient safety dashboard measures the percent of employees who have been educated on Stop the Line.*

To complement the survey process, and to measure and improve patient safety across the organization, the Office of Patient Safety uses biennial site visits to explore facility culture with respect to patient safety. Site visits are compared to a health "checkup" rather than a regulatory visit, which could be viewed as punitive. The purpose is to validate patient safety survey results and identify best practices for dissemination across the system, as well as discuss facility-specific patient safety concerns that require follow-up. Site visits are preceded by a detailed data review by the site visit team. This review and the site visit findings are summarized in a formal document describing good and best practices to share with other BSWH facilities and opportunities for improvement. This document is sent within ten business days of the site visit. The facilities then provide the Office of Patient Safety a formal report within eight weeks.

Patient safety site visits include separate focus groups with medical staff, managers/supervisors, and frontline staff; leadership meetings with staff at director-level and above; visits to units/departments (day and evening shifts); and a closing discussion with senior leaders (Kennerly et al. 2011). A patient safety site visit agenda is presented in Figure 2.9. Sample site visit questions are presented in Figure 2.10. The patient safety site visit team includes system leaders from Patient Safety, Risk Management, Patient Experience, Human Resources, Health Care Improvement, Informatics, Pharmacy, and Laboratory.

	Example BSWH Patient Safety Site Visit Program Agenda Entity and Date	
Patient Safety Site Visit Team	Vice President of Patient Safety Director of Patient Safety Director of Human Factors Nursing Analysis Champion, Patient Safety Quality Process Improvement Consultant, Patient Experience Executive Assistant Patient Safety Manager of Patient Safety Health Care Improvement Representative Informatics Representative Human Resource Representative Infection Prevention and Control Representative Accreditation and Regulatory Representative Pharmacy Representative	
Agenda		
Time	**Session/Room Location**	**Facilitator**
8:30–9:45	**Introductory Leadership Meeting** (Directors and above) *Location:*	Vice President of Patient Safety
10:00–11:30	**Focus Group Sessions:** Group I: Managers and Supervisors *Location:*	2–3 Patient Safety Site Visit Team Members for each session
10:00–11:30	Group II: Frontline Staff *Location:*	
10:00–11:30	**Visit with Staff in Work Areas/Units/Departments**	2–3 Patient Safety Site Visit Team Members
11:45–1:00	**BSWH Patient Safety Team Meeting and Lunch** *Location:*	Patient Safety Site Visit Team
1:00–1:30	**Closing** (Senior Leaders) *Location:*	Vice President of Patient Safety

This is an example of the possible participants and agenda for the Patient Safety site visit. Depending on the size of the facility, this would determine the number of participants.

Figure 2.9   Example patient safety site visit program agenda.

BSWH Office of Patient Safety
Patient Safety Assessment Program—Questions for Unit/Department Visits or Focus Groups

Facility: Unit/Dept._____   or Focus Group _____   Shift _____   Team Member(s)_____

Questions and topic suggestions are designed to comfortably solicit feedback from staff and are intended to start the conversation. Team member visiting with staff is free to let staff express safety concerns on any topic. Summarize themes/trends in categories provided.

What is going well regarding Patient Safety?	Culture of Safety	Regarding patient safety on your unit	Other	Follow up on actions from last site visit or unit/department specific concerns to address.
– Unit initiatives – Process Improvement projects – National Patient Safety Goals – Lean projects – Best Practices	– Speaking up – Stop the Line – Event Reporting – Event Reporting Follow Up – Patient Safety Leadership activities – Chain of Command/Resolution	what keeps you up at night or is the "pebble in your shoe" and what would you suggest as a solution?	– Low value tasks – Teamwork – Communication – Safety and Security – Equipment – Staffing – Disruptive or violent behavior – Electronic Health Record	

Please summarize the feedback and format into the categories below that can be included in the facility report.

Leadership:

Strengths/Good Practices:

Opportunities/Concerns:

Evidence of Teamwork/Effective Communication:

Strengths/Good Practices:

Opportunities/Concerns:

Resources:

Strengths/Good Practices:

Opportunities/Concerns:

Reporting & Feedback:

Strengths/Good Practices:

Opportunities/Concerns:

Other:

Strengths/Good Practices:

Opportunities/Concerns:

RECOMMENDATIONS:

Figure 2.10   Example patient safety assessment program questions.

Conclusion

The second step in the journey toward safer patient care involves the creation of a culture in which all members of the organization are accountable for patient safety, work to achieve patient safety aims, and drive patient safety initiatives. To develop this culture, the organization needs to be transparent about its patient safety goals and progress toward achieving them. In addition, organizational leaders should demonstrate their commitment to patient safety and transparency by recognizing and rewarding employees who "speak up" to prevent errors or enhance patient safety. Another important element of a patient safety culture is continuous communication of ideas, best practices, and opportunities for improvement; this communication is facilitated by Patient Safety WalkRounds and TalkRounds and Patient Safety Officer Huddle Calls. Finally, the use of an organizational patient safety culture survey supported by site visits enables leaders to understand areas of strength and opportunities for improvement in the organization's patient safety culture.

Chapter 3

Integrating the Culture

After an organizational culture of patient safety has been created, this culture will need to be integrated across departments and disciplines. An integrated culture of patient safety will be characterized by interdisciplinary collaboration and the use of more complex analysis and measurement tools to support implementation of patient safety initiatives. During this step of the patient safety journey, BSWH created an annual plan that tied health care improvement and risk management to patient safety, developed a department dedicated to infection prevention and control, expanded its work related to risk management, and used approaches and analyses derived from human factors to enhance patient safety (see Figure 3.1).

Annual Plan—Health Care Improvement, Risk Management, and Patient Safety

To advance its patient safety aims and initiatives and foster interdisciplinary collaboration, BSWH has committed to the development and implementation of an Annual Plan for the departments of Health Care Improvement, Risk Management, and Patient Safety. The Plan supports the vision of BSWH "to be the most trusted name in giving and receiving safe, quality, compassionate health care." With the Plan, the organizations' four areas of focus (quality, service, people, and finance; see Chapter 1) are used to establish and prioritize goals and to monitor clinical and operational effectiveness. To hardwire excellence into the performance improvement process, engaged leaders commit to excellence and select process

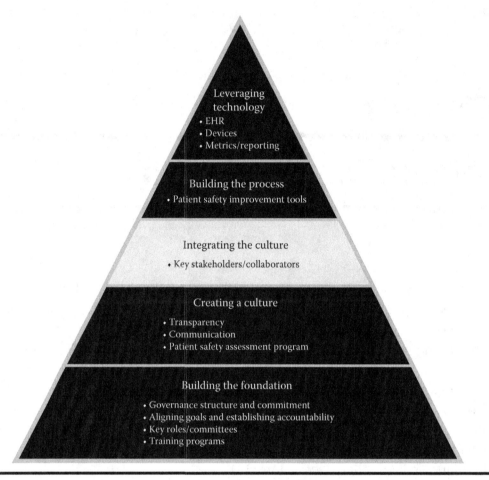

Figure 3.1   Patient safety framework for achieving safe health care. EHR, Electronic health record.

and outcome metrics while building a learning culture around service and safety. Leaders promote transparency, accountability, and mutual respect, with a focus on employee satisfaction and aligning behaviors with goals and values. To ensure that all components of the organization are integrated into and participate in the Plan, the roles and responsibilities of the Board, Medical Executive Committee, senior leadership, Health Care Improvement, Risk Management, and Patient Safety, and other various teams and committees are outlined below.

The Board of Trustees has ultimate responsibility for the provision of optimal performance improvement throughout the organization. The Board delegates to the Medical Executive Committee, board members, medical staff, and senior leadership of BSWH the operational responsibility for performance improvement as follows:

a. Provide direction in setting patient safety, risk management, and performance improvement priorities based on the BSWH mission, vision, values, and strategic goals
b. Oversee the design, implementation, and ongoing monitoring of the organization-wide improvement function
c. Establish an organizational culture that supports a commitment to patient safety, risk management, and performance improvement
d. Provide adequate resources, both material and personnel, to accomplish patient safety, risk management, and improvement functions
e. Receive, review, and accept reports regarding the effectiveness of organization-wide patient safety, risk management, and improvement functions

Key positions and their corresponding responsibilities and functions as outlined by the Plan are described in Table 3.1.

Table 3.1   Annual Plan Key Positions, Responsibilities, and Functions

Key Positions	Responsibilities and Functions
Baylor Scott & White Health (BSWH) Operations Board	a. Accountability and leadership for the Plan b. Delegates responsibility for implementation of the Plan to the Medical Executive Committee (MEC) and senior leadership c. Uses information and findings to identify patterns/trends and identifies opportunities for improvement d. Reviews, evaluates, and approves the Plan, annually e. The Operations Board • Ensures that the quality assessment and performance improvement program reflects the complexity of the hospital's organization and services; • Involves hospital departments and services (including those services furnished under contract or arrangement); and • Focuses on indicators related to improved health outcomes and the prevention and reduction of adverse errors.

(*Continued*)

Table 3.1 (Continued)   Annual Plan Key Positions, Responsibilities, and Functions

Key Positions	Responsibilities and Functions
MEC	The MEC is accountable for the safety and quality of care, treatment, and services in the hospital/clinic. Representatives of the MEC a. Review the patient safety (PS), clinical risk management (CRM), and quality/health care improvement (HCI) activities impacting patient outcomes and provide support for organization-wide improvement activities b. Have representation on the Quality/HCI/CRM/PS committee(s) c. Approve the Plan d. Involve medical staff members in improvement activities including peer review or focused evaluation of professional practice e. Assist in the development of systems to identify, correct, and evaluate specific causes of potential risk f. Participate and champion PS initiatives g. Ensure that the quality assessment and performance improvement program incorporates the hospital departments and services, including contracted services
Senior leadership	a. Provide support and authority to Quality/HCI/CRM/PS personnel to function effectively b. Provide internal processes and activities throughout the organization related to quality and safety and continuously and systematically measure, assess, and improve care, treatment, and services c. Provide guidance in establishing priorities for PS, CRM, and quality projects based on best practices and prioritization and methodology d. Allocate resources for assessing and improving PS, CRM, and quality/HCI e. Implement processes including peer review and performance evaluations of employees to address behaviors related to quality, safety, and risk management f. Analyze and assess the effectiveness of contributions to PS, CRM, and quality/HCI

(*Continued*)

Table 3.1 (Continued)   Annual Plan Key Positions, Responsibilities, and Functions

Key Positions	Responsibilities and Functions
Quality/HCI/ CRM/PS BSWH Committee	The Quality/HCI/CRM/PS Interdisciplinary Committee designated to manage the organization-wide quality, CRM, and PS initiatives is responsible for the following tasks: a. Drafts and distributes the Plan format for facility use, annually b. Recommends projects across BSWH requiring multidisciplinary teams c. Oversees, assesses, and supports the multidisciplinary PS, CRM, and facility teams d. Designs and plans cross-functional and multidimensional improvement activities across the organization e. Reviews feedback from Patient Satisfaction Surveys, PS and CRM data, Infection Control reports, and other executive level data/information impacting patient quality and safety f. Assesses the effectiveness of the PS, CRM and Quality/HCI activities of the hospital/clinic departments and teams g. Determines the education and training needs of the organization related to PS and quality h. Determines budget implications of organization-wide PS, CRM, and quality/HCI activities
Quality/HCI/ CRM/PS Hospital/Clinic committee(s)	Quality/HCI/CRM/PS committee(s) a. Develop and implement methods for identification, evaluation, and prevention of issues, which may cause injuries to patients by recommending strategies for loss prevention including but not limited to, guideline development, modification, and/or deletion b. Review and evaluate trended events and risk data identified through the event reporting software for improvement opportunities c. Confidentially review and evaluate Identified individual occurrences and sentinel events, conduct root cause analysis, and implement lessons learned d. Review risk issues identified through claims and patient events, for PS and HCI opportunities

(Continued)

Table 3.1 (Continued)   Annual Plan Key Positions, Responsibilities, and Functions

Key Positions	Responsibilities and Functions
	e. Evaluate potential risk exposure/PS issues and make recommendations for resolution f. Identify risk areas for educational opportunities and refer identified issues to the appropriate individual, facility committee, performance improvement committee, committee performing peer review, or other medical staff committee g. Designate ad hoc members for the purpose of executing committee activities, recommendations, and duties h. Review and evaluate BSWH STEEEP Best Care initiatives and determine applicable implementation strategies i. Engage in proactive risk assessments j. Collect quality, safety, and clinical risk data on contracted services and report annually to the MEC
Hospital/clinic staff and support personnel	a. Staff participation in performance improvement teams is essential because frontline team members have the most knowledge of actual day-to-day processes b. Every employee should participate in PS and quality activities c. Employees are provided education on performance improvement and PS in hospital/clinic orientation, departmental orientation, departmental meetings, and/or in ongoing educational programs d. Tactics used to promote awareness of PS may include, but are not limited to , Safety and Quality Fairs; monitoring compliance to National PS Goals; staff orientation and skills lab; and communication through staff meetings, lessons learned, newsletter, flyers, huddle boards, and posters e. Each hospital/clinic department will have a systematic, ongoing process for monitoring, evaluating, and improving the quality and cost-effectiveness of the care or service provided; participate in HCI, customer service, and PS activities after identifying priorities; and comply with accreditation and regulatory requirements for improving organizational performance as it applies to the specialty
Contracted services: hospital/clinic (contractee) and contractor	a. The hospital/clinic develops, implements, and maintains an effective, ongoing, facility-wide, data-driven quality assessment and performance improvement program for contracted services b. Contracted services adhere to the hospital/clinic's processes and perform in the same manner as hospital/clinic staff and support personnel. These expectations are to be shared in the contract negotiations between the two entities

Infection Prevention and Control

A BSWH infection prevention and control specialist describes preparation efforts to treat patients with Ebola after the first confirmed case was diagnosed in the United States on September 30, 2014.

As a health care system, we were notified that a patient with a confirmed diagnosis of Ebola was in the community. We learned that a proactive, team approach was important in managing this situation. From an infection prevention and control perspective, some items to evaluate include the following:

1. *Consider how the infection prevention and control leaders will work with the organization to quickly mobilize resources to manage and respond to media, community, and regulatory inquiries.*
2. *Consider how the infection prevention and control leaders will work with the organization to manage and respond to internal staff inquiries and to communicate with employees across the system.*
3. *Consider a regular, daily (if beneficial) huddle with key leadership to review and develop, as necessary, policies and procedures to address an Ebola-type situation. This could include equipment availability, training and education, employee safety, and patient safety.*
4. *Develop a plan to keep up with Centers for Disease Control and Prevention recommendations.*
5. *Broaden this model to address other high-risk infectious diseases.*

To integrate a culture of patient safety across the organization and its various departments and disciplines, a department dedicated to infection prevention and control should be established. This department will oversee the surveillance and reporting of outbreaks of nosocomial infections and will put in place and monitor the results of processes to prevent the transmission of infectious diseases (Kohn et al. 1999). Among the department's most important responsibilities will be the measurement, monitoring, reporting, and prevention of health care-associated infections (HAIs). According to the Centers for Disease Control and Prevention (CDC), on any given day, about 1 in 25 hospital patients have at least one HAI. There were an estimated 722,000 HAIs in U.S. acute care hospitals in 2011. About 75,000 hospital patients with HAIs died during their hospitalizations, and more than half of all HAIs occurred outside the intensive care unit (Magill et al. 2014).

At BSWH, the Infection Prevention and Control Department's purpose is to minimize the mortality, morbidity, and economic burden associated with HAIs through prevention and control improvement activities in both patient and staff populations. Using evidence-based principles, the team collects and analyzes pertinent data to determine risk factors associated with infection and to define mechanisms of transmission. The infection prevention specialist uses this information to seek opportunities for improvement and then plans, implements, and evaluates control strategies. As a resource within the facility and the community, the infection prevention specialist educates other professionals as well as the public about infection risks and measures to reduce and/or minimize risks. Some key initiatives and components of the department's strategy are described in the following.

Hand hygiene:
- Hand hygiene is one of the most important means of preventing the transmission of infectious agents (CDC).
- Per BSWH's Hand Hygiene Protocol, health care providers should decontaminate hands upon entry into and exit from all patient rooms.
- For hand decontamination, alcohol-based hand rub or soap and water may be used.
- Hands must be washed with soap and water when hands are visibly soiled or after exposure to *Clostridium difficile.*

Prevention of intravascular catheter related blood stream infections:
- Hand hygiene actions should be performed before line insertion and before each time the line is accessed.
- Maximum barrier precautions should be used at every central venous catheter insertion (i.e., large sterile drape should be used; health care provider should wear surgical mask, sterile gloves, hair covering, and sterile gown).
- The subclavian vein is the preferred site for nontunneled catheters in adults.
- Skin should be prepped with chlorhexidine before insertion.
- Use of femoral site should be avoided unless it is an absolute necessity to use it.
- A daily review of line necessity should be performed.

- The health care provider should "scrub the hub" (i.e., clean the injection port) vigorously before each time the line is accessed.
- Timely dressing changes should be performed using aseptic technique, with chlorhexidine disk placed at insertion site.
- Chlorhexidine daily bathing should be performed for adult critical care patients.
- Coated catheter technology should be utilized.

Prevention of catheter-associated urinary tract infections:

- Health care providers should strictly adhere to aseptic insertion technique, with appropriate hand hygiene and gloves.
- Indwelling catheters should be used only when medically necessary and removed when they are no longer needed.
- Closed sterile drainage should be maintained.
- Strict adherence to proper catheter care should be maintained.
- Catheters or drainage bags should not be changed at fixed intervals.

Prevention of ventilator-associated pneumonia:

- The Hand Hygiene Protocol should be followed.
- Oral care with chlorhexidine should be provided.
- The head of the bed should be elevated to a minimum of thirty degrees at all times to prevent aspiration.
- Deep venous thrombosis prophylaxis techniques should be used.
- Stress ulcer prophylaxis techniques should be used.
- Endotracheal tube with subglottic suctioning should be used.
- Patients should be provided with a daily sedation vacation.

Prevention of multidrug resistant organism transmission:

- The Hand Hygiene Protocol should be followed.
- A gown and gloves should be donned at time of entry to patient's room.
- Decontamination of the environment should be performed.
- Methicillin-resistant *Staphylococcus aureus* (MRSA) active surveillance screening should be performed for designated high-risk populations.
- Contact precautions should be followed for all colonized and infected patients.
- Antimicrobial stewardship principles should be followed.

Prevention of surgical site infections:

- Prophylactic antibiotics should be used appropriately.
- Appropriate hair removal should be performed.

– Postoperative serum glucose should be controlled for surgery patients.
– Preoperative infection prevention education should be provided.

The BSWH Surgical Site Infection Surveillance Worksheet is displayed in Figure 3.2.

Surgical Site Infection Surveillance (SSI) Worksheet
Baylor Scott & White Health

Facility _____
SSI type _____
Met criteria?   Y   N

Patient MR#:	Died: N Y – Date: _____
Patient Acct #:	Adm: DC:
Patient Name: Last: First:	Middle:
Gender: F M	Date of Birth:
Date of Surgery: Date of Event:	Organism(s):

Event Details:

Specific SSI Event: □ Superficial □ Deep   □ OSI Procedure Type: _____ SSI contributed to death? Y   N
Detected: □ A (During admission)   □ P (Post-discharge surveillance) □ RF (Readmission to facility where procedure performed)

SUPERFICIAL INFECTION CRITERIA:

Infection occurs within 30 days after any NHSN operative procedure,
and
involves only skin and subcutaneous tissue of the incision
and
patient has **at least one** of the following:
___Purulent drainage from the superficial incision;
___Organisms isolated from an aseptically-obtained culture of fluid tissue from the superficial incision;
___Superficial incision deliberately opened by a surgeon, attending physician** or other designee
    and is:
        ___culture-positive or   ___not cultured
                    and
        patient has **at least one** of the following signs or symptoms:
        ___pain ___ tenderness ___localized swelling ___redness ___heat
        (Note: *A culture-negative finding does not meet this criterion*);
Diagnosis of a superficial incisional SSI by the surgeon or attending physician or other designee.

NOTE: *Diagnosis/treatment of cellulitis (redness/warmth/swelling), by itself, does not meet criterion for superficial incisional SSI. An incision that is draining or culture (+) is not considered a cellulitis.*

DEEP INFECTION CRITERIA:

Infection occurs within 30 or 90 days after the NHSN operative procedure
and
involves deep soft tissues of the incision (e.g., fascial and muscle layers)
and
patient has **at least one** of the following:
___Purulent drainage from the deep incision.
___ A deep incision that spontaneously dehisces or is deliberately opened by a surgeon, attending physician, or other designee, and is:
        ___culture-positive or   ___not cultured
                    and
        patient has **at least one** of the following signs or symptoms:
        ___Fever (>38°C) ___ localized pain or tenderness
        (Note: *A culture-negative finding does not meet this criterion*);
___An abscess or other evidence of infection involving the deep incision that is found:
        on direct examination, ___during invasive procedure, or ___by histopathologic examination or imaging test.

For DEEP and ORGAN/SPACE Surveillance:
Procedures with 90 day surveillance time frame: BRST, CARD, CBGB, CBGC, CRAN, FUSN, FX, HER, HPRO, KPRO, PACE, PVBY, RFUSN, VSHN

ORGAN/SPACE INFECTION CRITERIA:

Infection occurs within 30 or 90 days after the NHSN operative procedure
and
infection involves any part of the body, excluding the skin incision, fascia, or muscle layers, that is opened or manipulated during the operative procedure
and
patient has **at least one** of the following:
___Purulent drainage from a drain that is placed into the organ/space
___Organisms isolated from an aseptically-obtained culture of fluid or tissue in the organ/space
___An abscess or other evidence of infection involving the organ/space that is found:
        ___on direct examination, ___during invasive procedure, or ___by histopathologic examination or imaging test.
and meets at least one criterion for a specific organ/space infection site*

Which organ space definition was met? (i.e. IAB, GIT, BONE)

Revised 1/2015

Figure 3.2   BSWH Surgical Site Infection Surveillance worksheet.   *(Continued)*

**Surgical Site Infection Surveillance
(SSI) Worksheet
Baylor Scott & White Health**

*Specific sites of an Organ/Space SSI:

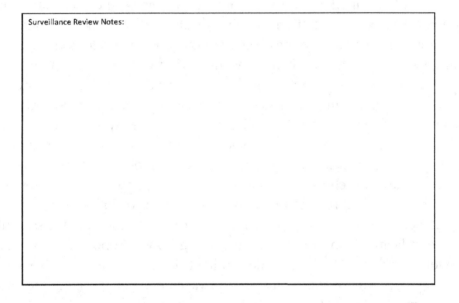

Code	Site	Code	Site
BONE	Osteomyelitis	LUNG	Other infections of the respiratory tract
BRST	Breast abscess or mastitis	MED	Mediastinitis
CARD	Myocarditis or pericarditis	MEN	Meningitis or ventriculitis
DISC	Disc space	ORAL	Oral cavity (mouth, tongue, or gums)
EAR	Ear, mastoid	OREP	Other infections of the male or female reproductive tract
EMET	Endometritis	OUTI	Other infections of the urinary tract
ENDO	Endocarditis	PJI	Periprosthetic Joint Infection
EYE	Eye, other than conjunctivitis	SA	Spinal abscess without meningitis
GIT	GI tract	SINU	Sinusitis
HEP	Hepatitis	UR	Upper respiratory tract
IAB	Intraabdominal, not specified	VASC	Arterial or venous infection
IC	Intracranial, brain abscess or dura	VCUF	Vaginal cuff
JNT	Joint or bursa		

Surveillance Review Notes:

Revised 1/2015

Figure 3.2 (Continued)   BSWH Surgical Site Infection Surveillance worksheet.

Influenza Vaccination Campaign

The Infection Prevention and Control Department should be dedicated to preventing and controlling infectious disease in both patient and staff populations. One notable case study regarding successful infection prevention among health care system staff is the BSWH Influenza Vaccination Campaign. In its early years, the campaign strongly encouraged employees to be vaccinated for influenza and provided free influenza vaccinations as well as education about the influenza vaccine. In 2007, the campaign was led by an interdisciplinary planning committee that included nurse leaders and designated "flu vaccination teams" at each hospital. Each team was headed by the site's employee health nurse. Enough vaccine was available for 90% of employees, and a sharing program was coordinated so facilities with less vaccine could receive additional supplies from sites with more vaccine. A list of priority groups for vaccination was designated in case of a pandemic.

The CDC-recommended slogan "Protect Your Patients, Protect Yourself" was adopted and included in education and marketing materials (i.e., flyers, posters, stickers, e-mails, intranet marketing, newsletters, and a computer-based learning module). Hospital leaders spoke about the vaccination campaign at numerous system-wide events, sent e-mails to staff regarding the importance of vaccination, and were pictured receiving the vaccination in marketing materials. All staff, including part-time and contracted employees and volunteers, were required to complete the mandatory computer-based learning module on flu vaccination. At the end of this module, employees were asked about their intentions for receiving or declining the vaccine. The vaccination schedule was provided through the intranet website, bulletin boards at facility entrances, and e-mails. Vaccines were offered during all shifts and on weekends at various locations to all employees, including part-time and contracted staff and volunteers. Mobile carts traveled to high-volume areas such as cafeterias, nursing units, and entrances; new staff orientations; and departmental meetings. To ensure workplace safety, safety needles and disposable sharps containers were used. Additionally, screening for contraindications and instruction regarding how to report adverse reactions were provided. Nurses assigned to light duty, nursing supervisors, and emergency department staff delivered the vaccine. After receiving the vaccine, staff were given "I Got My Flu Shot" stickers.

Employee health nurses recorded statistical data and sent periodic reports to the Office of Patient Safety. Vaccination statistics were compiled for each facility. Information was shared with each facility-level influenza vaccination team during the season so that areas with lower vaccination rates would be followed up to provide encouragement. Postcampaign assessment evaluated reasons for declination after completion of the mandatory computer-based module. This information was evaluated and used to plan the following year's immunization program. As a result of this initiative, in 2008, BHCS was recognized by the American Nurses Association as a Best Practice Organization for instituting an innovative program in seasonal influenza immunization for health care personnel (Slavin 2008).

Today, BSWH still has a policy requiring all employees to be vaccinated for influenza, a best practice for infection prevention. To obtain leadership buy-in for the mandatory influenza vaccine policy, the Infection Prevention and Control Department educated organizational leaders about the high rates of influenza mortality and morbidity that patients can experience when employees are unvaccinated (Ahmed et al. 2014). In 2009, the H1N1 (swine flu) pandemic occurred, further underscoring the need for strong prevention measures related to influenza. In 2012, BSWH began requiring its employees to be vaccinated as a condition of employment, and now, the organization has a 100% compliance rate with the vaccination policy.

The campaign required a strong interdisciplinary effort and included collaboration among diverse departments, including the Office of Patient Safety, Human Resources, Public Relations, and the Legal Department. To lead the mandatory influenza vaccination efforts, an executive committee established policies and procedures that addressed such questions as the following: How do we track which employees received the vaccine? How do we get the word out that the vaccine is mandatory? What qualifies an employee for an exemption from the mandatory influenza vaccination policy? Where do we allow employees with exemptions to work? What forms are needed for exemptions? What proof do we obtain if an employee has received the vaccine elsewhere? This committee ensured that education about the mandatory vaccination policy began eight months before the vaccines began to be administered. In addition to the executive committee, an interdisciplinary exemption review panel was established and included representatives from the Legal Department, Human Resources, Infection Prevention and Control, Patient Safety, and Pastoral Care.

One lesson learned from the first year of the mandatory influenza vaccine was the importance of having enough vaccination sites, staff, and supplies such as consent forms available early in the vaccination season. In the first year of the mandatory influenza vaccine, many employees came to the vaccination sites during the first three weeks, and staff were not prepared to vaccinate so many employees at once. In subsequent years, a team was established to interact with the Employee Health Department to ensure that enough staff, supplies, and locations were available for timely employee vaccine administration early in the season.

To prevent the spread of influenza, patients and hospital visitors as well as employees need to be educated about precautions to take if they think they might have influenza. Figure 3.3 displays a sign used across BSWH facilities during the 2014/2015 influenza season that educates patients about

IF YOU HAVE ANY OF THESE SYMPTOMS:

Fever	Fatigue
Body Aches	Runny Nose
Cough	Chills
Sore Throat	Headache

We want to keep everyone safe and healthy.
Please place a surgical mask over your
mouth and nose and notify staff. **THANK YOU.**

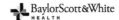

Figure 3.3   Sign for patients with symptoms of influenza.

how they can prevent the transmission of influenza. A version of this sign
was also available in Spanish.

Risk Management

The Risk Management Department plays an important role in supporting a
culture of patient safety. BSWH has a system-wide policy outlining procedures for reporting adverse events and disclosing events to patients and their
families, if applicable. This policy emphasizes the organization's commitment
to being open and honest with patients and families in sharing information.

As part of the Sentinel Event Alert process, the BSWH Risk Management
leads a facility-level gap analysis to determine next steps to address these
types of alerts.

One program that supports employees who make difficult disclosures or
deal with unexpected or traumatic patient outcomes is the BSWH Swaddle
program. The Swaddle team is composed of selected staff from various
backgrounds who have been trained in active listening and providing psy-
chological first aid. Team members provide peer support with complete
confidentiality. Employees who would like Swaddle team support can call or
email the group, discuss options for peer support, and be matched with a
qualified peer support volunteer. The Swaddle program helps to facilitate the

delivery of safe patient care by ensuring that staff receive appropriate support when necessary.

One principle of risk management is that adverse events resulting from errors that reach a patient do not generally happen as the result of a single source of error or failure; instead, more than one source of error or system failure typically occur together to cause such events. The need for several errors or failures to "line up" to cause an adverse event is referred to as the Swiss cheese model (Reason 2000) of accident causation. All members of the organization are accountable for patient safety, and everyone should look for potential sources of error and process or system failure and find ways to correct these and ensure safe patient care.

Human Factors

Human factors is the scientific discipline concerned with the understanding of interactions among humans and other elements of a system and is the profession that applies theory, principles, data, and methods to design to optimize human well-being and overall system performance. Human factors specialists contribute to the design and evaluation of tasks, jobs, products, environments, and systems to make them compatible with the needs, abilities, and limitations of people (International Ergonomics Association). The BSWH Human Factors department includes in-house human factors specialists who are involved in key safety process improvements such as electronic health record improvement and new facility design. The Patient Safety Department also provides education programs about human factors for leadership and key clinical councils. Human factors specialists are committed to understanding work in context, as experienced by frontline care providers, and integrating multiple levels of the socio-technical system to develop and deploy solutions that improve patient safety (Xiao and Probst 2014).

Key human factors principles include the following:

1. Anticipate human errors

A patient in labor at a hospital needed to use the bathroom. The father-to-be unhooked the patient from her monitors and helped her to the bathroom. When she returned to bed, he attempted to reconnect her to the monitors. The automated blood pressure cuff fit perfectly into the patient's intravenous (IV) line port. A nurse discovered the misconnection moments before the automated blood pressure cuff would have pushed air into the patient's IV port, potentially causing a fatal event. To prevent such events, BSWH "forces function" by using blood pressure tubing that is impossible to connect to an IV port.

Human error is inevitable and will never be eliminated; therefore, human factors experts gather data about "human characteristics and human interactions with the work environment" to design systems and tools that support physical and cognitive abilities of humans and are resilient to unanticipated events (Russ et al. 2013; Saleem et al. 2009). One example of this is error proofing of equipment through "forcing function."

2. Observe actual work processes

In many hospitals, sterile water bags used in respiratory therapy can easily be confused with normal saline bags intended for IV administration (Figure 3.4). IV administration of sterile water can have severe consequences for patients. At BSWH, after observation of storage of the two types of bags, human factors specialists recommended that sterile water bags be replaced with bottles. They confirmed that water bottles could be used with all hospital equipment and that their use was acceptable according to the organization's policies and procedures. They then interviewed nurses and respiratory therapists to assess the feasibility of using bottles for sterile water and to identify barriers to their use. Findings showed that staff preferred water bottles to bags because bottles could be ordered in a larger size; however, some respiratory therapy equipment lacked a pole on which to hang a bottle. Human factors specialists contacted the vendors of the respiratory therapy equipment to evaluate the potential of adding a pole to every ventilator, presented their findings to the Respiratory Therapy Council, and recommended the change from sterile water bags to bottles. After the council approved the change, human factors specialists created an education and notification plan for nurses and respiratory therapists about the enhancements to protect our patients.

Figure 3.4 Sterile water bags and normal saline bags.

Traditionally, when an error or near-miss occurs, patient safety officers and risk managers perform a Root Cause Analysis (RCA) to understand why the event occurred and how it can be prevented in the future. At BSWH, human factors specialists encourage the observation of actual work processes to support RCAs because a neutral observer with a fresh set of eyes may detect things that are overlooked by staff who perform the work every day. Observers note workflows, sequences of tasks, barriers to completing work, interesting or unexpected issues, staff strategies and workarounds to complete work, and policies and standards that staff must follow. The human factors observation cycle is presented in Figure 3.5.

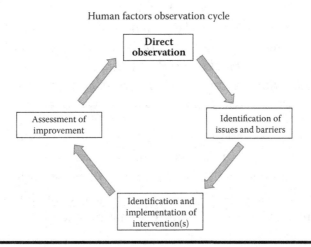

Figure 3.5   Human factors observation cycle.

3. Simplify visual design to make reading easier

*The Agency for Healthcare Research and Quality presents the
following case study from a U.S. hospital as an example of how
reading errors can lead to patient harm: A 43-year-old woman was
admitted to an intensive care unit with symptoms of heart and
respiratory failure. She was found to have severe mitral and tricus-
pid valve regurgitation. She responded well to medical therapy,
and surgical repair of her valve was scheduled. During her initial
evaluation, a jaw fracture was incidentally noted. Given the jaw
fracture and her valvular disease, an oromaxillofacial surgeon
recommended prophylactic antibiotic coverage before surgery.
Penicillin, 500 mg orally four times daily, was ordered. On the
second day of antibiotics, when the nurse compared the drug with
the medication administration record, she noticed that the patient
was receiving penicillamine (a nonantibiotic medication used in
the treatment of Wilson's disease and severe rheumatoid arthritis)
instead of penicillin and alerted the pharmacy.*

*A pharmacist reviewed the original handwritten order and saw
that penicillin was clearly prescribed. The pharmacist who entered
the order into the pharmacy computer system had typed in the
code "PENIC" and had received a drop-down box that displayed
all formulations and dosages of both penicillin and penicillamine.
That pharmacist had incorrectly selected penicillamine as the drug
to be given. The final check of the medication (at the time the
drug left the pharmacy) compared the drug product against the
information in the pharmacy computer system but not against the
original handwritten order. The patient suffered no ill effects from
the error and received the course of penicillin as originally prescribed (Agency for Healthcare Research and Quality, Morbidity
and Mortality Rounds on the Web: A Troubling Amine).*

When reading, people often scan to locate relevant information, seek
out and focus on specific items of information for a task, and develop
routines to rapidly locate information and to ignore information that
is rarely used. When creating forms and instructions, it is important to
anticipate and prevent reading errors that may lead to patient harm.
Several human factors principles applied to list making are illustrated in
Figure 3.6.

Human Factors Principles in List Making

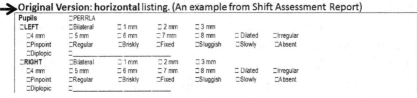

> We do **NOT** read word by word, from left to right.
> We tend to scan and compare, and are very sensitive to spatial arrangement

➤ **Original Version: horizontal** listing. (An example from Shift Assessment Report)

Pupils	☐PERRLA					
☐**LEFT**	☐Bilateral	☐1 mm	☐2 mm	☐3 mm		
☐4 mm	☐5 mm	☐6 mm	☐7 mm	☐8 mm	☐Dilated	☐Irregular
☐Pinpoint	☐Regular	☐Briskly	☐Fixed	☐Sluggish	☐Slowly	☐Absent
☐Diplopic	☐_____					
☐**RIGHT**	☐Bilateral	☐1 mm	☐2 mm	☐3 mm		
☐4 mm	☐5 mm	☐6 mm	☐7 mm	☐8 mm	☐Dilated	☐Irregular
☐Pinpoint	☐Regular	☐Briskly	☐Fixed	☐Sluggish	☐Slowly	☐Absent
☐Diplopic	☐_____					

➤ **Revised: vertical** listing. Information is grouped to support scanning

Pupils	☐PERRLA	☐Asymmetric				

LEFT					
☐Regular	☐Briskly	☐Absent	☐1 mm ☐5 mm		
☐Irregular	☐Slowly	☐_____	☐2 mm ☐6 mm		
☐Dilated	☐Sluggish		☐3 mm ☐7 mm		
☐Pinpoint	☐Fixed		☐4 mm ☐8 mm		

RIGHT					
☐Regular	☐Briskly	☐Absent	☐1 mm ☐5 mm		
☐Irregular	☐Slowly	☐_____	☐2 mm ☐6 mm		
☐Dilated	☐Sluggish		☐3 mm ☐7 mm		
☐Pinpoint	☐Fixed		☐4 mm ☐8 mm		

Spacing   Group   Vertical listing
                related items

Figure 3.6   Human factors principles in list making.

4. Improve teamwork and communication

> *While using the Universal Protocol for Preventing Wrong Site, Wrong Procedure, and Wrong Person Surgery, an operating room specialist noticed a discrepancy in the consent for surgery during the initial time-out process before a procedure began. The employee implemented Stop the Line and requested clarification before proceeding with the surgery preparation. The patient's paperwork was reviewed and the correct site was clarified. "As a result of the employee's swift action and attention to detail, the patient experienced a safe surgery," says the hospital's clinical risk manager and patient safety officer. "This is a true testament to how effective Stop the Line is."*

Safer patient care depends on effective communication within health care teams, but barriers to communication and teamwork exist. For example, different members of the team (e.g., a surgeon, an anesthesiologist, and a nurse on a surgical care team) may perceive teamwork differently. Team members may be unaware of their influence on other members of the team, may be reluctant to "speak up," or may rush to complete tasks without thinking about the importance of teamwork and keeping patients safe. To mitigate these barriers, BSWH human factors specialists encourage the use of communication techniques such as critical language (Stop the Line; see Chapter 1) and structured communication with SBAR (situation, background, assessment, recommendation; see Chapter 4), as well as the creation of a culture in which anyone will raise patient safety questions in a timely manner because it is their responsibility to do so and because they know they will be heard without facing negative consequences for speaking up.

The BSWH Human Factors Department is involved in a wide variety of initiatives to improve patient safety through the enhancement of work systems. Examples of these projects are presented in Figure 3.7.

Examples of Recent Human Factors Projects

Patient Safety Improvement
- Improving smart pump compliance
- Preventing wrong expressed breast milk in NICU
- Sterile water safety (ventilator use)
- Patient identification in ORs ("OR Passport")
- Prevention of tube misconnection in ORs (in CV surgery)
- Patient fall prevention in hybrid OR
- Contamination risk reduction during sterile processing
- Revision of surgical checklists
- Reducing alarm fatigue
- Patient wristband redesign
- Pharmacy medication label redesign
- Pharmacy cart-refill process redesign
- Human Factors "101" learning modules
- Crash cart redesign
- OCH medication reconciliation
- L&D infant banding process

Nursing: Improving worksystem
- Nursing efficiency improvement toolkit
- Implementing efficiency toolkit
- New facility design
- Nursing mobility pilot
- McKinney Mission Control pilot

Informatics
- Usability of EHR modules for falls, HAPU, and lines-tubes-drains
- Usability of physician ordersets
- Usability of sepsis screening tools
- EHR user experience improvement
- Usability of KBMA interface & roll out
- Nurse-pharmacist electronic communication
- Barcode med admin hardware checklist
- EHR downtime analysis
- Usability of suspend orders; medicated drips
- EHR metrics team participation
- EHR patient header redesign
- Infrastructure rounding

Innovation
- Consistent surgical teams
- Game-based nurse–physician communication learning tool
- CUSP & Learning board
- Accelerating nursing competency development

Figure 3.7   Examples of BSWH human factors projects.

Human Factors Case Study:
Bar-Code Medication Administration

Medication errors occur frequently in hospitals throughout the United States and can lead to patient harm (Brennan et al. 1991). Bar-code medication administration (BCMA) can reduce medication errors by as much as 40% (Poon et al. 2010), but reports of unintended consequences of BCMA implementation have been reported in the literature (Koppel et al. 2008). To prevent these unintended errors and consequences and maximize the safety benefits of BCMA, human factors methods can be used during BCMA go-live.

The Human Factors Department used a multidisciplinary team to guide the development of a BCMA implementation checklist at BSWH. The team included patient safety leaders, human factors specialists, physician and nurse leaders, leaders and staff from respiratory and pharmacy departments, and nursing and pharmacy informatics experts. The team was tasked with the implementation and activation of BCMA after performing a failure mode effects analysis. The team also developed postimplementation processes for reporting errors, measuring scanning compliance, and tracking process improvements. Human factors methods utilized included ethnographic observations, staff interviews, and usability evaluations of the BCMA interface. From these data, the team identified high-priority work system elements for successful BCMA implementation, developed an implementation checklist to be completed by every unit at all hospitals, anticipated barriers in workflow from process changes, identified potential staff inefficiencies from new technology and hardware, and identified potential patient safety issues related to expected staff workarounds. The implementation checklist is displayed in Figure 3.8.

Usability barriers addressed as a result of this checklist included the need to add or relocate hardware, maximize available space, optimize workflows, and eliminate inefficiencies resulting from unit layout. Usability barriers were packaged into staff training through collaboration with the EHR education team. This training included the practicing of difficult use cases, tips for interacting with alerts, and strategies for addressing expected points of confusion.

BCMA Implementation Infrastructure Readiness Assessment Checklist

Instructions:

The Baylor Health Care System BCMA Implementation Readiness Assessment Checklist is comprised of 3 sections of concerns: inpatient rooms, medication rooms, and workstation on wheels (WoWs). In order to better assess the readiness of your facility's infrastructure for go-live, we ask that you complete this checklist for each care area where BCMA will be utilized (one checklist per care area).

Scoring:

For each 'Yes' response, a point is given. There are no points awarded for a 'No' response. In order to calculate a score for each section, simply total all 'Yes' responses and fill in the associated 'Score' cells. The total number of 'Yes' values can be summed to create a global score when all sections are complete. The maximum score is 15 (the maximum score for each section is 5); with a higher score indicating a more thorough BCMA infrastructure assessment.

Facility: _____

Area of Care (please circle one): Med/Surg Tele ICU NICU PACU L&D Postpartum Dialysis

BCMA Implementation Infrastructure Readiness Assessment Checklist	Yes	No
Inpatient Rooms (for workstations installed at the bedside)		
Has *every unit* been evaluated for an installation location individually, including isolation rooms, accounting input devices (e.g. dongle, mouse, keyboard)?		
Have mock-up BCMA workstations been evaluated in the different identified locations and use scenarios evaluated (e.g. facing the Pt, avoiding family/visitors, etc)?		
Has the ergonomic adjustability of the BCMA workstation been considered?		
Does the area immediately surrounding the BCMA workstation contain adequate space for users to spread out and scan, prepare (e.g. crush), and sort medications?		
Have alternative computers been secured for situations in which the primary BCMA workstation is broken or malfunctioning?		
	Score: ____	
Medication Rooms		
Has the workflow of how nurses retrieve medications been mapped and evaluated?		
Was the option of profiling the Omnicells evaluated?		
Is there a process for storing medications that are not profiled in the Omnicell?		
Is a computer workstation readily available and located next to the Omnicell?		
Has the storage and charging processes of the BCMA scanners been evaluated?		
	Score: ____	
Workstation on Wheels (WoWs)		
Has the need for a WoW, environmental considerations (e.g. door width, in-room space, carpet halls, etc), and *all* WoW: staff ratios been evaluated (i.e. RN and RT)?		
Have the WoW requirements *of each unit* been evaluated (e.g. battery charging stations, extra batteries, WoW storage, network connectivity, etc)?		
Have infection control issues (e.g. disinfecting the device) been evaluated?		
Do the WoWs have adequate space for medication preparation (e.g. crush), administration (e.g. scanning), and storage (e.g. lockable drawers)?		
	Score: ____	
Global Score: ____ out of 15		

Human Factors @ Baylor Scott & White Health ©2014

Figure 3.8   BCMA implementation checklist.

Conclusion

After a foundation for safe patient care has been established and a culture has been created in which all members of the organization are accountable for improving patient safety, the culture needs to be further enhanced to integrate different disciplines and departments into driving the patient safety program. Interdisciplinary collaboration is crucial during the third phase of the patient safety journey, as are the creation and implementation of more complex plans and processes for measuring and improving patient safety. Tools for this phase of the patient safety journey may include a formal annual plan that aligns health care improvement and risk management to patient safety, while infrastructure may include departments dedicated to infection prevention and control, risk management, and human factors. Together, these departments, disciplines, and individuals will work to integrate the culture of patient safety into the fabric of the organization, helping to confidently move forward into the fourth phase of the patient safety journey, when building the process will become the focus.

Chapter 4

Building the Process

A comprehensive patient safety program requires strategies focused on culture, processes, and technology. Until this point, the journey to safer patient care has involved the building of a strong foundation for safe care and the creation and integration of a culture of patient safety. The fourth step in the journey will incorporate these improvements into efforts to develop and sustain specific processes that drive patient safety. Examples of such processes include mortality reduction initiatives, strategies and tools to improve communication, patient safety huddles, strategies to engage patients in the journey to safer care, and initiatives focused on specific service lines such as ambulatory care, cardiovascular care, and surgical care (see Figure 4.1).

Mortality Reduction

In order to "put a human face" on data related to patient safety efforts, the BSWH Board of Trustees often hears stories from patients and their families. In 2006, the board viewed a video presenting the story of grateful patient and her husband, who describe how her life was saved by a rapid response team. Rapid response teams—critical care teams that can be called by any staff member or family member who has a concern about a patient's condition—were implemented throughout the organization as part of its participation in the 100,000 Lives Campaign. The video, as a powerful example of how safety initiatives impact the lives of patients and their families, was distributed throughout the organization at Town Hall meetings and on the employee intranet.

As described in Chapter 1, the creation and implementation of an organizational patient safety program begins with an official commitment to safety from the highest levels of leadership. The BSWH Board of Trustees formally affirmed its longstanding commitment to patient safety in 2005, after the IHI launched its 100,000 Lives Campaign to save 100,000 lives over 18 months through six patient safety interventions (use of RRTs, delivery of evidence-based care for AMI, prevention of adverse drug events through medication reconciliation, prevention of central line infections, prevention of surgical site infections, and prevention of VAP). The 2005 board resolution committed the organization to implementing the six interventions and established a goal to reduce the inpatient mortality rate by at least 4% over the next year.

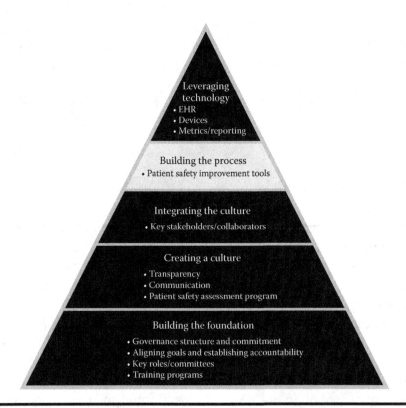

Figure 4.1   Patient safety framework for achieving safe health care. EHR, Electronic health record.

Empowered by this resolution, the organization's facilities, departments, and staff began to develop, implement, and measure the improvement associated with a variety of specific patient safety initiatives aligned with the resolution and the 100,000 Lives Campaign.

As part of the BHCS vision of "no preventable deaths," reducing inpatient mortality across our health care system remains an important objective. The BHCS Mortality Task Force was chartered in May 2009 to provide a more standardized approach for hospital-level review and improvement strategies.

Until fiscal year 2013 (FY13), BHCS was able to achieve a significant mortality reduction every year using the hospital-standardized mortality ratio (HSMR)-TX metric to guide improvement efforts (Figure 4.2). The HSMR-TX is calculated as the observed deaths divided by the expected deaths, with the latter determined from the mean performance of acute hospitals in Texas for the most recent year for which data are available. For FY13–FY14, the risk adjusted HSMR-TX mortality metric was proven not to be a reliable metric for facilities to focus their mortality improvement efforts due to the expected mortality rate in hospitals dropping significantly when physician documentation in the EHR was implemented. This unexpected measurement issue made this metric undesirable to demonstrate the risk-adjusted HSMR-TX method as a meaningful metric. BHCS then moved to measuring crude mortality rate (calculated using inclusion/exclusion criteria) for two high-risk areas:

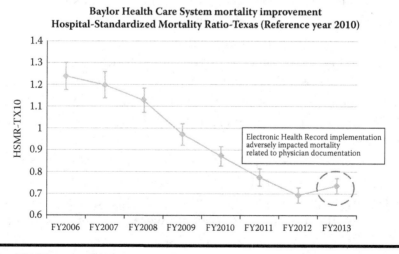

Figure 4.2   BHCS mortality improvement.

- Severe sepsis + shock
  - Emergency department (ED) focus on early recognition and management of sepsis patients by timely administration of antibiotics, fluid bolus, and expediting patient transfer to the inpatient setting
  - Utilization of a Code Sepsis team to assist with the ED care of these very complex patients in the ED
- Ventilator care
  - Engaged Critical Care Council facilitated this work
  - Ventilator checklist encouraged communication between disciplines and prompted evidence-based interventions
  - Intensivist coverage and further improvement work around sedation vacation (i.e., assessments where sedation is weaned off on hemodynamically stable patients to assess extubation readiness), spontaneous breathing trials, mobility, nutrition, and scheduled huddles/rounds were key areas to improve patient outcomes

Additional strategies and tactics for reducing mortality included the following:

- Multidisciplinary improvement teams (facility level) engaged in mortality case review (nurse, physician, Patient Safety Officer, care coordination, social work, health information manager, administration).
- System-level mortality cochair group that made decisions related to mortality goals and improvement initiatives met monthly to review system and facility performance, and invited facilities to discuss the barriers they were facing as well as improvement strategies (those not on track for meeting their mortality goal).
- BHCS Mortality Task Force met every two months to showcase improvement work in sepsis care, ventilator mortality, oncology, and other pertinent topics. Each facility presented its improvements and identified barriers. The group shared ideas for improving patient outcomes for a given topic.
- Reduction of referrals of patients to BHCS when recovery was not possible or not desired by patients/families.
- Palliative Care and Hospice Care were very active in the mortality reduction work to ensure that patients were receiving the most appropriate and supportive care for their disease process.

As part of the current BSWH vision of "no preventable deaths," reducing inpatient mortality across our health care system remains an important objective.

Communication Improvement

Patient safety improvement depends on strong communication among members of the health care team. A variety of tools, programs, and strategies have been developed to enhance this communication and foster an organizational culture in which patient safety is everyone's responsibility and priority. Examples of these strategies and tools include the Comprehensive Unit-Based Safety Program (CUSP), learning boards, structured communication through SBAR (situation, background, assessment, recommendation), Teamwork Improves Patient Safety (TIPS), and bedside shift reports.

Comprehensive Unit-Based Safety Program

Developed by Johns Hopkins University with funding from AHQR, CUSP encompasses a wide range of patient safety tools and approaches based on the understanding that culture is local and that work to improve culture must be owned at the unit level (Agency for Healthcare Research and Quality, *CUSP Toolkit*). The AHRQ modular CUSP toolkit includes training tools and resources that make care safer by improving the way physicians, nurses, and other clinicians work together. Toolkit modules include the following:

- Learn about CUSP
- Assemble the Team
- Engage the Senior Executive
- Understand the Science of Safety
- Identify Defects Through Sensemaking
- Implement Teamwork and Communication
- Apply CUSP
- The Role of the Nurse Manager
- Spread
- Patient and Family Engagement

Developed based on the principle that frontline staff have unparalleled knowledge about patient safety risks and how to address them, CUSP drives frontline staff accountability for improving processes and systems that positively impact patient safety.

In 2010, patient safety representatives from BSWH held a conference call with CUSP experts from Johns Hopkins University to learn how best to plan and implement CUSP initiatives. This meeting produced several key ideas for patient safety improvement:

■ Fall prevention: A unit clerk participating in a CUSP meeting suggested that unit clerks be responsible for checking the list of patients at high risk for falls against the list of beds with an activated alarm status. The clerk could check the two lists from his or her desk because the alarm status was accessible centrally at the nursing station.

■ A three-pronged approach to medication safety: prevention, capture, and recovery. As an example of prevention, several BSWH facilities were improving infusion safety during patient transport by ensuring adequate time remained in IV bags before transport.

In addition to these key ideas, two of the most important benefits of CUSP were identified and discussed:

1. Learning by senior executives about the impacts of their decisions on frontline staff (e.g., on budget)
2. Engagement of frontline care providers in proactively making the system safer, instead of passively reporting data

After this conference call, BSWH set a goal to adopt, modify, and spread CUSP throughout the organization, engaging frontline staff in a grassroots safety program that would allow professionals to work on safety hazards identified by the team to be of importance; provide a forum in which to develop a synergistic culture of empowerment, ownership, and accountability for brainstorming, problem solving, learning, and sharing; and improve patient safety and teamwork. The OPS developed a spread model that involved a "train-the-trainer" approach to facilitate system-wide implementation. Tools and resources were developed and posted in a "CUSP Toolkit" on the OPS intranet website.

The first program was deployed in a cardiovascular ICU with strong executive leadership and physician champion support. Early planning sessions were held with the leadership team to discuss the spread model. The unit manager held designated CUSP meetings every two weeks. The OPS provided patient safety, human factors, and science of safety expertise for meetings as needed.

One year after its start, dramatic improvements were observed for staff satisfaction scores (evidenced through specific National Database of Nursing Quality Indicators [NDNQI] data) and with results on the CUSP Safety Attitude Questionnaire, which measured the culture of safety. NDNQI scores improved from 2009 to 2010 as follows:

- Mean practice environment scale, 2.4 to 3.18 (scale 1–4)
- Job enjoyment, 46 to 61 (<40 = low, 60 = high)
- Percentage of unit nurses planning to stay in the unit, 64% to 90% (50%–100%)
- Perception of unit's quality of care, 3.28 to 3.67 (1–4)
- Would recommend hospital to friend, 3.9 to 5.14 (1–6)

The cardiovascular ICU CUSP team celebrated its first anniversary in April 2011 after demonstrating the true power of teamwork and problem solving. Not only did the team reduce patient safety hazards in the unit, but they also challenged themselves and the system by tackling larger issues that impact patients similarly in other ICUs throughout the organization. These results demonstrate that taking the time to develop a visible, well-structured unit program with strong, consistent facility and system leadership support will lead to continued, long-term success. Active involvement and support of the physician champion are important for navigating solutions for patient safety issues that may impact other physician practices, workflows, or service lines.

On the basis of this unit's success, the OPS produced a video to showcase unrehearsed clips from the staff, chief nursing officer, physician champion, unit manager, and director of education regarding their experience with the program. This video was posted on the OPS intranet website and was utilized to help others understand the impact of adapting the CUSP model in their units.

> *In one cardiovascular ICU, a nurse and an anesthesiologist used CUSP to create a checklist outlining their expectations for safe patient care both before patient transfer to the ICU and during patient admission to the ICU. The anesthesiologist says, "Physicians recognize that standardization is really important. For every patient, there are certain things we want to know—about their history, their physiology during the procedure that they just underwent, and what our major concerns are going forward in their immediate post-op interval. Getting that consistency and creating the right expectations for both the nurses and the physicians who care for that patient are important."*

Learning Boards

Learning boards are bulletin boards where frontline staff can post opportunities for patient safety improvement and track actions and achievements related to these opportunities. Learning boards can be placed in break rooms, as "minutes on the wall" that track progress and follow-up actions and resolutions, and in meeting rooms to support discussions and brainstorming. Learning boards enable staff to celebrate patient safety accomplishments and address remaining opportunities for improvement. At BSWH, managers and units that have implemented learning boards are encouraged to do the following:

- Number and record each card that is posted on the learning board.
- Place extra cards in multiple locations for staff use. Anyone can place a completed card on the board.
- Decide how the cards will be assigned and support the team to succeed. Achieving success engages staff to continue working through barriers and improve the process.
- Be creative. The board can be movable (with Velcro mounting) and can be taken to staff meetings, to the manager's office, or to small workgroup meetings. A good "home" for the board may be in the staff break room.
- Provide examples to staff of things to post on the learning board, such as "What is the pebble in your shoe?" or "What bugs you that you would like resolved?" or "How can the next patient be harmed?"

■ Consider incorporating the board into your unit's routine (e.g., in every morning huddle) to review progress regularly.

■ Use learning boards as an opportunity to "Show and Tell" all the great improvements that are happening in your unit when regulatory agencies visit or during patient safety rounds or other visits to the area.

A learning board template as well as an example learning board from an oncology unit are presented in Figure 4.3.

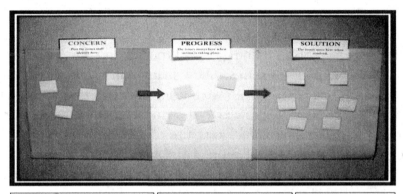

Staff post a card here	Card is moved to the section	Card is moved to the

– A quick description + date
– Examples:
  – Linen shortage on Monday morning
  – Documenting in different places for diaper rash in EHR
  – IV bags not labeled from OR transfer
	(with a date)
	– Claimed by staff member(s) to work on the issue
	– Support from managers other members
	– Status updated
		section when issues are resolved

Figure 4.3   Learning board template and example learning board from the oncology unit.

Situation Background Assessment Recommendation

Situation Background Assessment Recommendation (SBAR) is a form of structured communication, adapted from aviation and other reliable industries, in which one health care team member describes a patient's status to another team member by explaining the situation, background, assessment, and recommendation. SBAR promotes patient safety by encouraging the use of clear and focused communication in critical situations. This standard form of communication promotes exchange of pertinent information in a succinct format during critical situations. This method is especially effective on night/weekend shifts when there may be cross-coverage of physicians who are the least familiar with the patient.

BHCS implemented SBAR training of staff (nurses and physicians) in 2007. Clinician audits were performed to see how many staff had been educated on SBAR as well as the percentage who were using SBAR for critical communication. Physicians were also interviewed to determine whether the SBAR reports were adequate to make clinical decisions, use of the SBAR format, and whether they were the primary physician (Figure 4.4). Overall, SBAR was determined to be a communication tool that provides benefit, especially in critical situations. Some clinicians viewed this tool as a document (used in change of shift handoffs, transfers to other areas, etc.) instead of a communication technique.

The SBAR worksheet now used at BSWH, as well as an example SBAR scenario involving fall prevention, is presented in Figure 4.5.

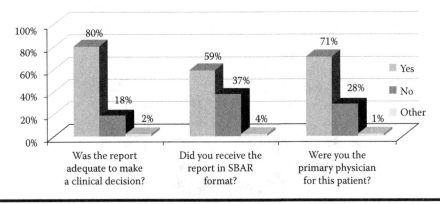

Figure 4.4   Results from physician interviews on SBAR.

Prepare for SBAR Communication:	
• Assess patient, take vital signs • Review chart for the appropriate physician to call • Know admitting diagnosis • Be aware of what has been going on with the patient for the last 12 hours (review progress notes; nurses notes) • When speaking with the physician have *available*: • Chart, Allergies, Medications, IV Fluids, Labs/Results • Take a moment to organize information, your thoughts, and the key message	
S (*Situation*) State • Your name/unit • Patient name; room number; attending physician name if calling on-call physician • The problem (if urgent, say so!) • Patient code status	I'm a physical therapist working with Mr. Smith in room 325 and he may be at risk for falls.
B (*Background*) State • Admission diagnosis and admit date • *Pertinent* medical history • Brief synopsis of treatment so far	He was alert when he came in yesterday, but has been more confused since returning from his procedure last night.
A (*Assessment*) State • What you think the problem or primary concern is • If uncertain, say so • Most recent vital signs • Assessment findings and changes specific to the issue • *Pertinent* therapies (IVs, O_2, etc.)	I discovered Mr. Smith trying to get up by himself even though I have told him many times this morning not to get up by himself. He could not tell me he was in the hospital.
R (*Recommendations*) • Express what you think the patient needs to address the problem Examples: • Transfer to higher level of care • Physician to come see patient within ___ (time) • Consultant to see the patient Request orders for tests, meds, treatments as needed	Would you like me to move Mr. Smith closer to the Nurses' Station and put the yellow fall precaution socks and wrist band on him?
Before Hanging Up: • Respectfully discuss/clarify plan or goal of care if orders not clear or you are uncertain if patient problem has been addressed. Chain of Command when needed. • **Read back** all verbal orders	

Document the assessment, notification of physician and outcome.

Figure 4.5 SBAR worksheet.

Teamwork Improves Patient Safety

The BSWH Teamwork Improves Patient Safety (TIPS) Program seeks to enhance teamwork through the improvement of communication skills that physicians and frontline staff need to respond to demanding patient care situations. In addition to teaching a variety of communication strategies, TIPS expands the concept of teamwork to include involving the patient and family members. In a typical 1.5-hour TIPS training session, participants accomplish the following objectives:

- Identify barriers to teamwork in the health care environment
- Discuss the role of communication in patient safety
- Describe the four elements of SBAR communication
- Define situational awareness
- Discuss how "Stop the Line" can be implemented in their units
- Describe effective teaching strategies (verbal and written) for patients with limited health literacy

Oversedation Initiative

Oversedation of patients in hospitals has been identified nationally as a significant patient safety risk (The Joint Commission, Sentinel Event Alert: Safe Use of Opioids in Hospitals). To prevent oversedation, leaders and staff at one BSWH facility formed the Breathe Team, an interdisciplinary team composed of quality leaders, patient safety leaders, risk managers, and frontline staff. Together, the team members developed a charter and identified potential vulnerabilities in processes that could result in patient oversedation and worked to correct these, using data to determine if a trend exists or if processes need to be further refined. In addition, the team created a video for frontline staff about oversedation and provided them with screening tools for preventing oversedation (Figures 4.6 and 4.7) and delivers ongoing training regarding sedation assessment. This team reports up to its facility Best Care Committee. The Breathe Team is a strong example of how teamwork improves patient safety.

Nursing Considerations and Monitoring For Patients Receiving Sedating Medications

- **B**e aware - sedation precedes opioid-induced respiratory depression.

- **R**efer to the *"Patient Safety Warning Sign"* and place in line of sight for family & visitors.

- **E**ducate patient, family/visitors
  - How to use PCA and PCA safety (no one but patient pushes button)
  - *Warning signs* to call immediately to nurse's attention
  - Rationale for waking patient for assessment of sedation level

- **A**LWAYS *validate 5 rights* of medication administration.

- **T**hink carefully about poly-pharmacy. Frequent or combined doses of sedating medicines can have a "stacking" effect leading to unexpected over sedation.

  Sedating Medications:
  - narcotics
  - anti-emetics (nausea)
  - muscle relaxers
  - sleepers
  - anti-anxiety
  - sedating antihistamines
  - consumption of home meds and/or narcotics during hospitalization

- **H**igh risk patients for respiratory depression may include:
  - Obstructive Sleep Apnea (known/suspected)
  - Obesity BMI $\geq$ 30
  - $\geq$60 years old

- **E**mploy warning devices such as apnea alarms, pulse oximetry or capnography which can alert practitioners to respiratory depression. If you suspect over sedation, contact the physician, RRT and anticipate the need for Narcan administration.

  > A change in the patient's behavior or level of consciousness may be an early sign indicating over sedation. This is often missed due to the perception that the patient is comfortably asleep and stable.

Minimum recommendations:
- Wake your patient up to evaluate level of pain, alertness, vital signs, rate and quality of respirations, especially those who show minimal response to speech and/or touch, every 2-4 hours, even at night. *More frequent assessments may be necessary* for high risk patients.
- You may need to wake your patient up for monitoring more frequently during the first 24 hours of PCA use, even at night. Especially if on a continuous infusion.

Figure 4.6 Nursing considerations and monitoring for patients receiving sedating medications.

Bedside Shift Report

The Joint Commission has identified communication failures during patient transitions in care as a common cause of sentinel events in the United States (The Joint Commission, *Sentinel Event Data: Root Causes by Event Type, 2004—Q2 2014*). To improve communication among members of the health care team and ensure safer patient care, BSWH uses bedside shift reports during the handoff of care from one caregiver to another during shift

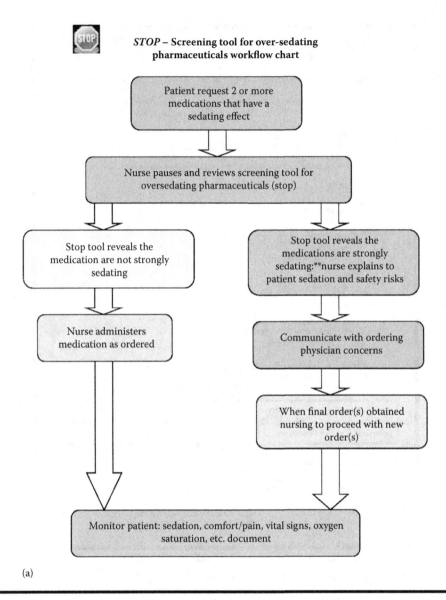

STOP – **Screening tool for over-sedating pharmaceuticals workflow chart**

(a)

Figure 4.7 **(a) Screening tool for oversedating pharmaceuticals.** *(Continued)*

changes or other transitions in care. Bedside shift reports involve the real-time exchange of information at the patient's bedside, which enables the patient and family to be involved in the conversation. This patient involvement increases accountability for continuity of care, helps to ensure patient safety and quality of care, and strengthens teamwork through transparent communication.

During a typical bedside shift report, the caregivers stand on each side of the bed, across from each other, and include any applicable equipment

STOP - Screening Tool for Over-sedating Pharmaceuticals
This list is NOT all inclusive, there are additional sedating medications not listed below.

Non Pharmacologic Interventions		Non-Sedating	Moderately Sedating**	Strongly Sedating**
Repositioning Reassurance Application of heat/cold Guidance Encouragement	Touch Massage Relaxation Deep breathing Music	Preferred	Use caution when administering with strongly sedating medications	Try to avoid administering 2 or more from this column

Opioids*
Peak
  IV 10 - 30 min
  PO 30 - 90min
  Transdermal 24 hours
Duration
  IV 3 – 4 hours
  PO 3 - 8 hours
  Transdermal 48 – 72 hours
				Buprenorphine (Suboxone)
				Codeine
				Fentanyl (Sublimaze)
				Hydrocodone/APAP
				Hydromorphone (Dilaudid)
				Methadone
				Morphine (MS Contin, Roxanol)
				Oxycodone (Oxycontin)
				Oxymorphone (Opana)

Anti-nausea Peak IV 10 - 30 min PO 2 hours Duration 16 hours		Ondansetron (Zofran)		Promethazine (Phenergan) Prochlorperazine (Compazine)
Muscle Relaxants Peak 3 – 4 hours Duration 18 hours			Methocarbamol (Robaxin) Metaxalone (Skelaxin) Baclofen	Carisoprodol (Soma) Diazepam (Valium) Cyclobenzaprine (Flexeril)
Sleepers Peak 2 hours Duration 9 hours			Zolpidem (Ambien) Zaleplon (Sonata)	Temazepam (Restoril)
Anti-histamines Peak 1 - 2 hours Duration 18 hours		Cetirizine (Zyrtec) Fexofenadine (Allegra) Loratidine (Claritin)		Diphenhydramine (Benadryl) Hydroxyzine (Atarax)
Anti-anxiety Peak 3 - 4 hours Duration 12 – 30 hours			Clonazepam (Klonipin) Alprazolam (Xanax)	Lorazepam (Ativan) Diazepam (Valium)
Miscellaneous		Tramadol (Ultram)	Scopolamine Patch Quetiapine (Seroquel) Gabapentin (Neurontin) Pregabaline (Lyrica) Amitriptyline (Elavil)	Meclizine (Antivert) Haloperidol (Haldol) Olanzepine (Zyprexa)

*Oral route preferred. May consider use of IV opioids, if ordered, 2 hours after oral for unrelieved pain OR if patient vomited oral opioid.
**Lower doses preferred. Consider staggering administration so medication sedating effects do not peak at the same time.

10.09.2013 cmc

(b)

Figure 4.7 (Continued) (b) List of sedating medications and alternatives.

needed for the handoff. This arrangement places the patient at the center of the process. The caregivers offer the patient the option to participate in the bedside shift report before the change of shift occurs. (This can be done by the departing caregiver during the final rounds before the shift change.) If the patient chooses to participate, the caregiver offers him or her the option to limit any information shared with guests present during the report. If the patient would like the report to be performed privately, then the caregivers invite guests to wait in the waiting area during the bedside shift report.

The caregivers' bedside shift report includes necessary medical history, physical exam results, updates from the shift, applicable test results, medication schedule information, and nursing orders. In addition, to ensure the highest levels of patient safety, the caregivers perform two-person visual checks on incisions, dressings, tubes, equipment, and skin integrity. They also update whiteboards to include the oncoming caregiver's name and any updates to the patient's care plan. A sample bedside shift report competency assessment form is displayed in Figure 4.8.

Bedside Shift Report Competency Assessment

		Observed	Comments
Unit:			
Date:			
Name of Caregiver:			
Evaluator:			
Offers option to participate in Bedside Shift Report (can be done before change of shift)			
Prior to medical information exchanged, asks guests to temporarily leave (can return in 10 min)			
If patient participates, offers option to limit any information shared with guests that are present			
Uses interpretive services as appropriate			
Introduces and manages up the oncoming caregiver			
Updates patient communication board in the room, to include date and caregiver names			
Gives a timeframe for how long report should take			
Explains what is taking place, to "keep you informed about your care", or "to include you in all decisions regarding your care and treatments"			
Checks name and armband before report begins, using key words "for your safety"			
Stands on each side of the bed across from each other, placing patient in center of report (if possible)			
Gives handoff report, including necessary history, exam, updates from shift, test results, medication schedule, and orders			
Performs 2-person visual checks (incisions, dressings, tubes, equipment)			
Uses applicable EHR, kardex and computer			
Invites patient into conversation; encourage patient to express concerns and questions			
Discusses plan for the day, including tests/procedures, medications, MD needs, and writes plans on the patient communication board			
Discusses new medications and side effects (also a teach-back opportunity)			
Addresses pain, treatment plan, options, goals, and writes on patient communication board			
Discusses discharge planning needs as appropriate (also a teach-back opportunity)			
Discusses with patient his/her goal for the shift, and writes on patient communication board			
Rounds on the patient, addressing the 5 Ps			
Thanks the patient and guests, asking if there is anything else we can do for them			
Oncoming caregiver gives a timeframe for when they anticipate returning			

Figure 4.8   Bedside shift report competency assessment form.

Bedside shift reports help to inform patients about their plan of care, allow patients and their families to witness a safe and professional transition of care between caregivers, and involve patients in their own care, decreasing the potential for errors and near misses.

Patient Safety Huddles

Huddles are more than just a process; they are a driver of a culture of patient safety. Their goal is to make the principles of safe, high-reliable care so hardwired throughout the organization that it becomes "second nature" for employees to follow these principles. A nurse leader at one BSWH facility describes the effects of this hardwiring: "I was walking down the hallway the other day and noticed an empty wheelchair sitting outside a patient's room. Before [learning about high-reliability principles], I might not have thought much about it. But I realized that the wheelchair might be in the way if someone needed to get into the room quickly, so I moved it. Another nurse saw me and said, 'Great attention to detail!'"

Several BSWH facilities use patient safety huddles to enhance communication among health care team members and drive the adoption and implementation of safer care processes. The purpose of these huddles is to improve patient safety through the application of five principles of high-reliability organizations:

■ Preoccupation with failure: Every employee is encouraged to constantly think about ways work processes could break down and address these potential problems before they occur.
■ Reluctance to simplify interpretations: High-reliability organizations dig deeply to find the source of a particular problem instead of assuming that problems have similar causes.
■ Sensitivity to operations: Each employee pays close attention to details of operations and maintains awareness of things that are or are not working well rather than making assumptions about what is or is not working well.
■ Commitment to resilience: High-reliability organizations are prepared to respond to failures and continually find new solutions.
■ Deference to expertise: Leaders at high-reliability organizations listen to people who have the most knowledge about a process or task regardless of how much seniority that person has (Weick and Sutcliffe 2001).

One BSWH facility has developed an especially robust model for patient safety huddles. The huddle occurs every morning at 9 a.m. and lasts 15 to 20 minutes; no other meetings can be scheduled during that time. A representative attends from every department and division in the hospital, as well as from the outpatient ambulatory care setting. The administrator on call leads the huddle to convey the message that everyone on the leadership team, whether a clinician or nonclinician, embraces and promotes a culture of safety. The leader asks the following five questions:

1. What happened during the last 24 hours that could impact patient safety?

    This question underscores the importance of communication and transparency regarding safe patient care. For example, if a near miss occurred during the last 24 hours, then everybody in the huddle will discuss the event, what caused it, and how it can be prevented from happening in the future.

2. What will happen in the next 24 hours that could impact patient safety?

Examples could include the introduction of a new procedure, an adjustment to workflow, a planned information technology (IT) down-time, or a call light that is scheduled to be repaired.

3. Are there any issues with equipment or staffing that need to be addressed?

The purpose of this question is to ensure that the hospital has enough resources to respond to issues identified in Question 2 that might arise in the next 24 hours. For example, if there is an IT down-time scheduled that day, then huddle participants will discuss back-up resources that will be deployed during that time to ensure the smooth delivery of safe patient care.

4. Were there any Great Catches during the last 24 hours?

As described in Chapter 2, Great Catches happen when an employee spots an error, problem, or safety risk before it reaches or impacts the patient. Discussion of Great Catches enables each huddle participant to consider how the potential safety risk could arise in his or her depart-ment and how it can be prevented.

5. Is there any patient in our facility now who wouldn't give us a score of 9 or 10 if we asked them about their satisfaction with their care?

If any such patients are identified, then leaders will round with them and ask them why they are not completely satisfied with their care. This rounding process involves patients in their own care and also enables leaders to learn about potential ways to improve the delivery of safe patient care.

Patient Engagement in Safety

Building effective patient safety processes throughout an organization requires the engagement of patients as part of the health care team. Patients and families should be encouraged to make recommendations about ways to improve safe care and should have opportunities to share their care experi-ences with health care team members and with the organization's leaders. A variety of initiatives have been developed to engage patients in safe care, including "Three Words" videos, the BSWH "Patient Safety Starts With Me" campaign, and patient and family advisors who make recommendations about ways to improve care.

Patient Safety Starts With Me

In 2007, BSWH began its "Patient Safety Starts With Me" campaign to foster a stronger partnership between patients and their health care teams. Through newsletters, posters, a video, and the employee intranet, frontline staff were encouraged to engage patients and families as the most important members of their health care teams. The OPS produced Patient Safety Tips cards in both English and Spanish, distributed them to staff, and displayed them throughout hospitals (Figure 4.9).

In addition to the Patient Safety Tips cards, the OPS used the "Patient Safety Starts With Me" initiative to help drive a patient safety culture in which staff not only communicate effectively with patients and their families but also engage them as the most important members of their own health care team (Figure 4.10).

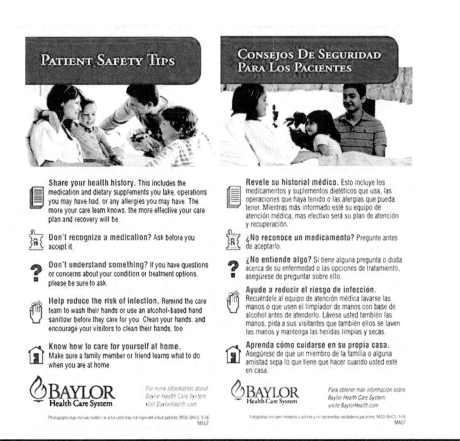

Figure 4.9   Patient safety tips cards.

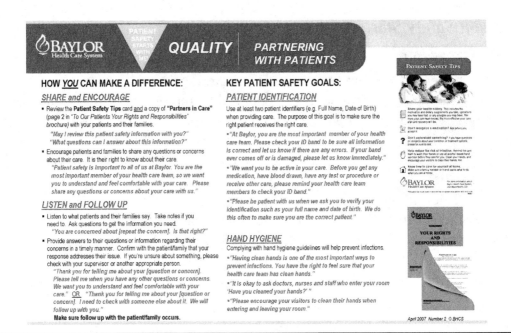

Figure 4.10   Patient Safety Starts With Me: Partnering with Patients.

Patient and Family Advisors

To further involve patients and their families in improving the delivery of safe health care, BSWH works with volunteer patient and family advisors. These advisors are recent patients or family members of recent patients who participate in a variety of organizational committees and councils focused on STEEEP care and patient safety. Advisor roles enable patients and families to influence the way care is organized and delivered and help to ensure that they have a voice in decisions and plans that affect patient care. Advisors may be involved in short-term projects, such as a task force to redesign an ED waiting room, or longer-term commitments, such as a two-year membership on a committee whose goal is to improve STEEEP care.

One BSWH hospital has a dedicated Patient and Family Advisory Council whose goal is to strengthen the health care team by providing constructive, practical advice and feedback to create an optimal and safe health care experience. Qualifications for council members include the following:

■ Strong communication and listening skills
■ Comfort with working with others and speaking in a group
■ Ability to communicate and work with families and staff with diverse backgrounds, experiences, and communication styles

- Positive and supportive attitude toward the organization's mission and vision
- Interest in the improvement process and in making a difference in patient care

All council members are required to attend a one-time volunteer orientation and meet the annual health and education requirements of the facility's Volunteer Department. Terms last two years and may be extended by the council's leaders. New council members partner with current members to review materials such as the orientation checklist, the council's charter, and the council's current list of activities and accomplishments. The objectives of the Patient and Family Advisory Council are as follows:

- To review and recommend ideas intended to improve the patient and family experience
- To function as an editing body for review of patient education materials to help ensure that all materials are accurate, comprehensive, and understandable
- To optimize patient care by eliminating or reducing barriers to patients and families having the ideal care experience

One example of the work of the Patient and Family Advisory Council is to help determine the most important elements to be included on each patient's whiteboard (Figure 4.11).

In addition to bedside shift reports, whiteboards in patients' rooms provide an overview of the patient's goals, needs, contact information, and targeted discharge date. Developed with input from the Patient and Family Advisory Council, these whiteboards focus attention on goals and needs that are important to each specific patient. Care providers can quickly scan these boards to learn about the most important aspects of the patient's care plan. Sample patient whiteboards are presented in Figure 4.11.

Another example of the work of the Patient and Family Advisory Council is the Patient/Family Workgroup Discharge Team established at one facility with the aim of decreasing negative comments by 50% for the inpatient discharge experience from unit to car. This initiative was a result of a patient who feared that the area presented an increased risk for falling and another patient who was very dissatisfied with lack of help getting belongings into the car. The team aimed to increase communication between all disciplines and patients and families, provide clear instructions, and improve

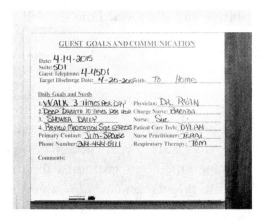

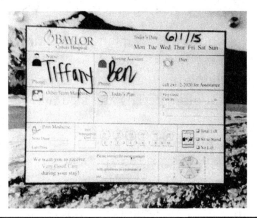

Figure 4.11 Sample patient whiteboards.

the aesthetics of the unit to achieve a safe and pleasant experience for the patient. This team achieved the following accomplishments:

- Improved transport staff education to include patient-centeredness training
- Achieved ongoing validation of expected behaviors of transport personnel
- Improved aesthetics of the discharge area (Figure 4.12)
- Developed standardized discharge map for facility (Figure 4.13)
- Established relationship with the Patient Transport leaders and staff
- Achieved goal of reducing negative comments from 7.6% to 2.7%

In addition to formal advisor roles, patients and families can be engaged in the improvement of safe care through more informal patient panels. At some BSWH facilities, patients with compelling stories related to STEEEP care are invited to tell these stories onstage at a meeting for physicians, frontline staff, residents, and students. Patients with especially notable stories

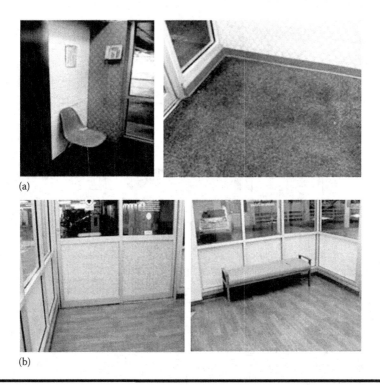

(a)

(b)

Figure 4.12   (a) Before and (b) after results of discharge improvement work.

are invited by organizational leaders to tell their stories at board meetings and at dinners with board members.

Through opportunities to serve in advisor roles and share stories with organizational leaders and frontline staff, patients and families become more involved in their own care and help to determine how safe care delivery can be improved.

Ambulatory Care

Developing and implementing common strategies and initiatives to drive safer patient care can be a challenge in the ambulatory care environment, where outpatient care—including diagnosis, observation, consultation, treatment, intervention, and rehabilitation services—may be delivered by multiple clinics and providers. HealthTexas Provider Network (HTPN), the BSWH-affiliated multispecialty medical group, has been a leader in the delivery of safe patient care since the group was first established in 1994. HTPN employs over 850 providers practicing in 250 care delivery sites in North Texas. It comprises seventy primary care centers, 180 specialty care clinics, and a family practice

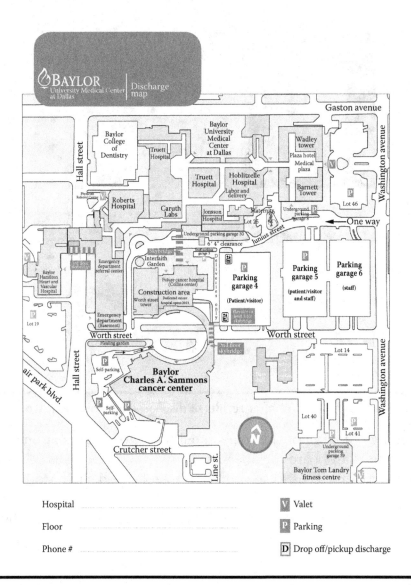

Figure 4.13 Discharge map.

residency program and reported more than two million patient visits in 2014. HTPN was awarded the American Medical Group Association (AMGA) Medical Group Preeminence Award in 2010 and was named an AMGA Acclaim Award Honoree in 2011, 2012, and 2014. Some of HTPN's strategies and initiatives to drive safe patient care are described in the following.

Ambulatory Care: Patient Safety Committee

As discussed in Chapter 1, the success of an organizational patient safety program depends on the infrastructure dedicated to improving patient safety. The mission of the HTPN Patient Safety Committee is "to contribute to attaining the HTPN goals by minimizing the risk of adverse events to patients by identifying issues that will lead to the implementation of both clinical processes and cultural initiatives." The Patient Safety Committee, like all HTPN committees, is chaired by practicing physicians and includes other members such as nurses, midlevel providers, and administrative staff. Its members are drawn from HTPN as well as from the BSWH OPS, ensuring that the patient safety goals of BSWH and HTPN are aligned. HTPN patient safety leaders also align the organization's patient safety program with national goals; for example, leaders from HTPN recently presented details of its program at a prominent national patient safety conference.

To build and sustain a patient safety program across HTPN, the Patient Safety Committee develops strategies and communication plans to reach physicians and other staff throughout all HTPN clinics and ensures that they are aware of current challenges and initiatives related to patient safety. It also develops communication, training, and evaluation programs to enhance its patient safety culture and develop and measure the success of patient safety processes.

Ambulatory Care: Patient Safety Pledge

One unique feature of the HTPN patient safety program is the Patient Safety Pledge (Figure 4.14). All HTPN employees are required to sign the Patient Safety Pledge promising to notify their patient safety representative of any unexpected events or near misses that occur while they are caring for a patient. The pledge promotes individual accountability for patient safety, allows employees to learn from each other's experiences, and enables patient safety leaders to identify and prevent potential errors and near misses before they occur.

Ambulatory Care: Patient Safety Rounding

The Patient Safety Committee adopted the concept of patient safety rounds based on the rounding techniques (WalkRounds and TalkRounds) used by the BSWH OPS (Chapter 2). HTPN patient safety rounds are conducted by a physician member of the Patient Safety Committee, the Director of Clinical Improvement, and the HTPN Manager of Patient Safety. Together, they visit individual clinics and hold meetings in three parts: (1) with employees but without managers, (2) with physicians, and (3) with managers and practice administrators. They ask questions about what is going well with respect to patient safety and what opportunities exist for improvement. Employees are

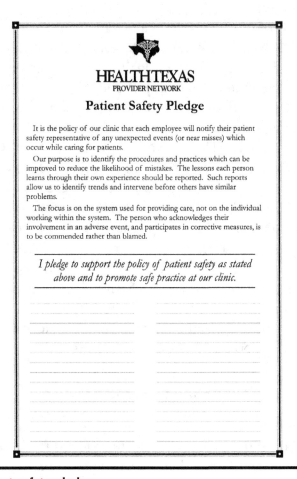

Figure 4.14   Patient safety pledge.

encouraged to speak freely and openly during rounds, and comments are kept anonymous to facilitate transparent sharing of ideas. To encourage staff to voice their concerns, note cards are provided to staff in case they want to write comments instead of sharing in the group. In addition, physicians from the committee often use examples from their own practices to "break the ice" and empower employees to speak up with examples and observations about how safety can be improved.

Ambulatory Care: Patient Safety Liaisons

Each HTPN clinic has a patient safety liaison (PSL), a peer resource and local expert on patient safety. Annual meetings are held for all PSLs, and the Patient Safety Committee uses various methods to educate PSLs, including slide shows, skits, interactive sessions, and games. At the annual meetings, as well as at other informal meetings throughout the year, PSLs are provided with opportunities to direct questions to the Patient Safety Committee members and network with PSLs from other clinics. HTPN has also created a newsletter specifically for PSLs and asked them to share this newsletter at their clinics to educate their peers. PSLs dedicate time in every monthly staff meeting to the discussion of patient safety issues. An example newsletter is presented in Figure 4.15.

March 2015 Volume 6, Issue 1

Patient Safety E -Newsletter

Infection Prevention in an Outpatient Setting

As more and more patients are seeking care in outpatient settings there is a need for greater emphasis on infection prevention. Patients with vulnerable conditions often use outpatient clinics to maintain or improve their health. It is critical that the care delivered protects, minimizes and reduces the risk of healthcare-associated infections.

So what can you do to help prevent the spread of infections in your clinic? First, you must have the appropriate equipment and supplies necessary to consistently maintain standard precautions. This includes:
- Hand Hygiene products
- Injection equipment
- Personal Protective Equipment (PPE) - gloves, gowns, face and eye protection

Second, ongoing education is critical for ensuring that infection prevention policies and procedures are understood and followed. HTPN has a hand hygiene policy that outlines when to use soap and water and when it is appropriate to use alcohol based cleansers. Policies should be reviewed and reinforced if there is a breakdown in maintaining appropriate hand hygiene. Also, HTPN requires that anyone in direct patient care not wear any type of gels, appliques, wraps or tips to the fingernail. These artificial nails trap bacteria that can be spread to patients. The HTPN hand hygiene policy can be found here: https://www.mybaylor.com/htpn/departments/patient_safety/Pages/forms.aspx

Third, we need to monitor and report healthcare-associated infections. Every year the state of Texas releases a list of notifiable conditions. https://www.dshs.state.tx.us/idcu/investigation/conditions/ This list should be reviewed annually in your clinic for any changes. Most recently, the list that came out in January 2015 includes that TB infection must be reported within 5 work days. This includes reportable tuberculosis infection following: a positive result from an Interferon-Gamma Release Assay (IGRA) test such as a T-SPOT or QuantiFERON-TB Gold In-Tube (QFT-G) or a tuberculin skin test (TST) plus a normal chest x-ray and asymptomatic patient. Since many of our clinics perform TB skin tests, if a patient tests positive these will now need to be reported to the state.

Fourth, we need to practice safe injection practices to prevent the transmission of infectious diseases. You will see on the next page that an injection was recently administered through a patient's clothing. This is never an acceptable practice. You must use aseptic technique when preparing and administering medications. Always cleanse the access diaphragms of medication vials with 70% alcohol before inserting a device into the vial.

Fifth, outpatient facilities should have policies and procedures in place for routine cleaning and disinfection of environmental surfaces. Patient exam tables should be wiped down with a Sani-cloth in between each patient. Equipment such as blood pressure cuffs should be cleaned if a patient has a rash or visible sores. Keeping surfaces free of food and drink in patient care areas is critical to the spread of infection. By following these guidelines we keep our patients safe and stop the spread of infection in the clinic.

http://www.cdc.gov/HAI/settings/outpatient/outpatient-care-guidelines.html

Figure 4.15   Patient safety newsletter.

Ambulatory Care: Orientation and Training

The HTPN orientation strategy for new staff is based on the premise that a culture of patient safety should be instilled from the first day of employment. To introduce this culture of patient safety to new employees, HTPN developed a clinical skills training program, which is required for all new clinical staff. Patient safety is discussed in every session of this program. Physicians and midlevel providers attend three full-day sessions during their first year of employment, and all three sessions address patient safety topics, including the following:

- Focus on development of culture
- Recognition of events and errors
- Standardization of processes when possible
- Effective and respectful communication
- Tracking system
- Abbreviation awareness
- Hand hygiene
- Patient activation
- Patient safety tips cards and posters
- Patient safety rounds
- Flu vaccination campaigns

These patient safety initiatives and concepts are continually reinforced through training, educational materials, posters, newsletters, and other communication vehicles. For example, HTPN developed and implemented a

Don't give bacteria a free ride.

Prevent infections by
practicing good hand hygiene.

Figure 4.16 Hand hygiene awareness campaign poster.

Hand Hygiene Policy similar to the policy used at BSWH (Chapter 3). The associated HTPN Hand Hygiene Campaign sought to raise awareness about the policy and remind employees about the importance of hand hygiene to patient safety. A campaign poster is displayed in Figure 4.16.

Ambulatory Care: Patient Safety Survey

To measure its patient safety culture, HTPN uses a modified version of the APPSS (Chapter 2) in its clinics. Like BSWH, HTPN surveys its employees. Data from the survey are reviewed and analyzed by the Patient Safety Committee, and the results are used to set priorities and goals. The survey is electronic and includes free-text areas so employees can comment on opportunities for improvement and ideas on how to resolve issues. Survey results are communicated to the BSWH Board of Directors and to the BSWH OPS, facilitating alignment of patient safety strategies and goals between BSWH and HTPN.

Ambulatory Care: Event Reporting

In accordance with the Patient Safety Pledge, employees must report patient safety events and near misses to their patient safety representative. During orientation, new employees are educated about how to report these events in the EHR and about the policy of nonretaliation for employees who report events and near misses. When employees submit an event report, they are instructed to include the following information:

■ A short summary of the event—include details such as the name and dosage of the medication, where the event occurred, and who was notified.
■ Always include a resolution—examples include "patient taken to the emergency department" or "patient will receive follow-up care with another provider."
■ Communicate to the patient if there was an error. If you gave the wrong medication or the wrong dosage, the patient needs to be aware of what happened. If you do not feel comfortable having this conversation with the patient, you can ask your supervisor to speak with them. Please make sure that you document this in the medical record.

HTPN patient safety leaders discuss event and near-miss reports with the Patient Safety Committee and develop strategies and policies to prevent these events from occurring in the future. For example, the HTPN "The

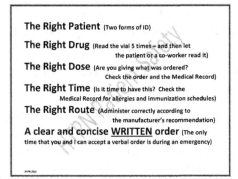

The Right Patient (Two forms of ID)

The Right Drug (Read the vial 5 times – and then let
the patient or a co-worker read it)

The Right Dose (Are you giving what was ordered?
Check the order and the Medical Record)

The Right Time (Is it time to have this? Check the
Medical Record for allergies and immunization schedules)

The Right Route (Administer correctly according to
the manufacturer's recommendation)

A clear and concise <u>WRITTEN</u> order (The only
time that you and I can accept a verbal order is during an emergency)

Figure 4.17   The Right Patient flyer.

Right Patient" flyer (Figure 4.17) was developed to prevent medication errors that could impact patient safety.

Ambulatory Care: Patient Engagement in Safety

Like BSWH, HTPN engages patients and families as an important part of the health care team and encourages them to speak up to improve patient safety. HTPN uses the Patient Safety Tips Card (Figure 4.12) as well as a variety of other initiatives to involve patients and families in safe care. One current initiative focuses on fall prevention for patients who have had an injection or blood draw. "Feeling Dizzy?" posters are displayed in HTPN

Figure 4.18   "Feeling Dizzy?" posters.

clinics in both English and Spanish to encourage patients to tell their health care provider if they have difficulty breathing, are feeling faint, or have an allergic reaction after an injection or blood draw (Figure 4.18).

Through the Patient Safety Committee and PSL roles; initiatives such as the Patient Safety Pledge, patient safety rounding, the patient safety survey, and event and near-miss reporting; and the engagement of patients and families as part of the health care team, HTPN ensures that a culture of patient safety is spread and sustained across its 250 diverse care delivery sites.

Cardiovascular Services

Examples of initiatives to develop and sustain processes that drive patient safety can be found in the BSWH cardiovascular service line, which uses a team-based approach to evaluate risk of mortality for cardiac surgery patients. For all elective cardiac surgeries, a surgeon performs a mortality risk assessment, and if the risk exceeds a certain level, then a second surgeon reviews the case. If the surgery is deemed high risk, then a team assessment is performed. Team members (e.g., interventional cardiologist, cardiovascular surgeon, nurse, anesthesiologist, social worker) sit down together and evaluate patient data such as laboratory tests, echocardiograms, and questionnaires that assess patient frailty and quality of life. Sometimes, surgeons will ask that team assessments be performed on low-risk cases. In addition, team evaluations are performed for every potential transcatheter aortic valve replacement patient (as required by CMS the Centers for Medicare and Medicaid Services [Centers for Medicare and Medicaid Services, *Decision Memo for Transcatheter Aortic Valve Replacement (TAVR) (CAG-00430N)*]). Team review of mortality risk before surgery helps to ensure the delivery of safe care by engaging the expertise of health care professionals from multiple disciplines.

To analyze the low incidence of mortality that occurs in cardiovascular service line patients, BSWH uses Phase of Care Mortality Analysis (POCMA), a systematic method of mortality review based on the following concepts: (1) all cardiac surgical deaths undergo a root cause of death analysis and (2) the clinical course of a cardiac surgery patient is a series of events, therapeutic decisions, interventions, and responses to treatment that are independent (Shannon et al. 2012). For each death, the analysis requires categorizing the mortality trigger into one of five time frames: preoperative, intraoperative, ICU, postoperative floor, and after discharge. With POCMA, surgeons,

Cardiac Surgery - Phase of Care Mortality and Morbidity Analysis**
(not Physician Peer Review activity)

MRN # _____   Surgeon_____

Transfer from another facility   Y   N   Emergency room admit   Y   N   Elective   Y   N

Procedure Performed _____   Pre Operative STS Risk of Mortality Score _____   If risk > 5% was second opinion obtained   Y   N
Case review –

PHASE OF CARE MORTALITY ANALYSIS: Please select PHASE and circle ONE or MORE subcategories that contributed the most to death

Pre-Operative Phase	Intra -Operative Phase	Post-Op ICU Phase	Post-Op Floor Phase	Discharge Phase
Cardiac Risk Factor CHF Cardiogenic Shock Myocardial Viability	**Anesthesia** Technical (lines, TEE, ET) Pharmacological management Recognition treatment of issues	**Hemodynamic Management** Inotrope titration Adequate O2 delivery	**Pharmacologic management** Coumadin Other	Appropriate disposition Pharmacologic details
Non-cardiac risk factors ≥ 2 major risks Renal Failure on Dialysis COPD Cerebralvascular Disease PVD	**Surgeon** Judgment Technical Myocardial protection	**Respiratory Care** **ICU Care** (keystone criteria) HOB elevate 30 degrees DVT prophylaxis Sepsis prevention Nutritional support Glycemic control PUD prophylaxis	**Surveillance/ recognition/Rx of decompensation**	Adequate instruction and support networks Catastrophic Event
Judgment Timing of Surgery Risk vs Benefit	**Cardiopulmonary By-Pass** Parameters Fluid management	**Surveillance/ recognition/Rx of decompensation**	**Sepsis prevention /treatment**	_____
Patient preparation Medical status optimized		**Catastrophic Event**	**Catastrophic Event**	_____
Patient evaluation Functional Class		_____	_____	
Other:				

As determined above was this event avoidable?	Was surgical death avoidable? Yes No
Yes No If yes how?_____	If yes, how _____
_____	_____
Relative strength this sentinel event triggered a fatal outcome	_____
Certain Most Likely Uncertain	(**Copy completed form via interoffice to BHCS-IHCRI: CV Serviceline Support, 8080 N. Central Expressway, Ste 900)

Figure 4.19   Cardiac surgery phase of care mortality analysis.

physicians, and hospital leaders determine the first event that led to the mortality and identify patient safety and quality improvement opportunities related to that first event. The POCMA form is presented in Figure 4.19.

The cardiovascular service line drives safe patient care through its systematic, multidisciplinary approach to evaluating mortality risk, determining the root cause of mortalities that do occur, and implementing improvements to prevent such events in the future.

Surgical Care

To improve the delivery of safe patient care, the BSWH surgical care service line has implemented several initiatives related to the World Health Organization (WHO) Safe Surgery Saves Lives (SSSL) checklist and associated timeout procedures.

Safe Surgery Saves Lives

The WHO launched the SSSL initiative in 2007 to reduce variation in surgical care (Haynes et al. 2009). BHCS piloted the checklist at eight hospitals and demonstrated improvements (Ballard et al. 2014). BHCS adopted a resolution to fully implement the WHO SSSL checklist in 2009 (Figure 4.20).

The SSSL checklist targets safety issues including effective surgical teamwork and communication, safe anesthesia practices, and prevention of surgical infections. Using the checklist requires team members to follow critical steps to reduce the risk of patient harm. Effective use entails the involvement and support of surgeons, anesthesiologists, nurses, and other team members, who are empowered to "Stop the Line" (Chapter 1) if they need clarification about any part of the procedure. The checklist identifies three distinct phases in a surgical procedure: before the induction of anesthesia, before skin incision, and before the patient leaves the operating room (OR). An example SSSL checklist is presented in Figure 4.21.

With this enhanced focus on teamwork and communication, BSWH created an enhanced surgical safety checklist process that clearly delineates which surgical team member is responsible for which action and includes specific actions related to fire safety (Figure 4.22). The anesthesia timeout is performed by the anesthesia provider and nurse in the OR before induction. The procedural timeout engages the whole team, and each team member has a speaking part; the team member who knows the information best delivers the information. The signout/debrief is performed by the team before the surgeon leaves the room to get everyone "on the same page" about what happened during the procedure and about the patient's

RESOLUTION
OPERATING POLICY AND PROCEDURE BOARD OF DIRECTORS

WHEREAS, attaining consistently reliable surgery is a cornerstone of providing safe care to a large fraction of Baylor patients; and

WHEREAS, the World Health Organization's Safe Surgery Saves Lives (SSSL) checklist has been shown to save lives and improve other outcomes for patients; and

WHEREAS, significant opportunities exist to more fully implement the WHO SSSL checklist in BHCS hospitals;

THEREFORE, BE IT RESOLVED, that the Operating Policy and Procedure Board of the Baylor Health Care System commits Baylor clinical and executive leaders to take all necessary steps to overcome barriers to implement the WHO SSSL checklist in all surgical procedures during the next six months; and

FURTHER RESOLVED, to report their progress quarterly in doing so until it deems sufficient success has been reached.

Figure 4.20   Board resolution to implement the SSSL checklist.

SURGICAL SAFETY CHECKLIST

SIGN IN (Before Induction of Anesthesia)
☐ Patient/designee has confirmed: patient, procedure, side and site, consent
☐ Site marked (or not applicable)
☐ Anesthesia safety check completed
☐ Anesthesia TIME OUT performed
☐ Allergies reviewed
☐ Difficult airway/aspiration risk addressed, and equipment/assistance available, if indicated
☐ Type & Crossmatch addressed

TIME OUT/PAUSE (Before Skin Incision)
☐ Confirm all team members have been introduced by name and role and actively participate
BRIEFING:
☐ Positioned and protected appropriately; surgical site marking visible after patient prepped and draped
☐ Implants/special equipment/supplies/instrumentation available
☐ Sterility (including indicator results) has been confirmed
☐ **TIME OUT** - Surgical team verbally confirms correct patient, procedure, side and site, consent
☐ **TIME OUT** - for new physician or new procedure
☐ Surgeon reviews: Critical steps, operative duration, anticipated need for blood products,
need to administer antibiotics or fluids for irrigation
☐ SCIP measures verified as appropriate
- Antibiotic prophylaxis
- VTE prophylaxis
- Hypothermia prevention
- Assess continuation of beta blockers
☐ Essential imaging properly labeled and displayed, if applicable
RN Signature: _____ Date: _____ Time: _____

SIGN OUT (Before patient leaves operating room)
RN verbally confirms with the team:
☐ The name of the procedure completed
☐ Instrument, sponge, and needle counts correct (or not applicable)
☐ All specimens appropriately labeled and sent (or no specimens)
☐ Whether there are any equipment or other problems to be addressed
☐ Surgical team reviews the key concerns for recovery and management
RN Signature: _____ Date: _____ Time: _____

Place original copy in patient chart; place copy in designated area in department

Legend: IV = intravenous; **kg** = kilograms; **mL** = milliliters; **RN** = Registered Nurse; **SCIP** = Surgical Care Improvement Project; **VTE** = Venous Thromboembolism

Figure 4.21 SSSL checklist.

postoperative plan. Fire risk is scored by the circulating nurse before the patient enters the OR.

In addition to the SSSL checklist, which engages all members of the surgical team, BSWH offers training and support for specific surgical team members. For example, one BSWH hospital provides an orientation for new anesthesiologists that involves meetings with key leaders, instruction in the EHR, and focused professional practice evaluation (Figure 4.23).

Because of the importance of surgical care to patient safety, the APPSS includes a question focused on the SSSL. Since 2009, staff members who work in surgical units have been asked to what extent they agree with the following statement: "The Safe Surgery Saves Lives (SSSL) process took place as well as you would like if you or a family member were the patient."

Figure 4.22 BSWH surgical safety checklist. ASA, American Society of Anesthesiologists Physical Status; CST, certified surgical technologist; EBL, estimated blood loss; FiO$_2$, fraction of inspired oxygen; ID, identification; MH, malignant hyperthermia; O$_2$, oxygen; RN, nurse; VTE, venous thromboembolism.

Employee Name: _____ Position: _____

To enable a smooth, safe and robust transition into practice at this hospital, the following orientation modules must be undertaken:

	Date completed	Employee's initials	Instructor's initials
Interview with Chief or Assistant Chief of Department			
Meet with Anesthesia Technician Director			
Meet with OR Director			
Meet with Biomed Leadership to confirm familiarity with anesthesia equipment or undergo in-service			
Meet with pharmacy staff to learn schedule drug procedures			
Meet with information services staff for electronic health record training and sign off			
Spend a minimum of first clinical day (MDs and CRNAs) doubled up with a senior staff person			
Cardiac anesthesiologists spend a minimum of first week in the cardiac operating rooms being proctored by staff anesthesiologist			
Placed on focused professional practice evaluation			

Employee Signature _____ Date: _____

Supervisor Signature _____ Date: _____

Figure 4.23 Orientation checklist for new anesthesiologists.

Starting in 2009, the OPS began implementing the following interventions to improve the culture of safety for surgical care:

■ Rounded with OR staff to determine barriers to compliance with the SSSL checklist
■ Monitored checklist compliance every 6–8 months by e-Survey
■ Increased OR staff competence and confidence in "stopping the line" if processes were not followed in the OR
■ Shared survey data with surgeons/OR team and recognized those surgeons, anesthesiologists, and team members who consistently complied with the checklist
■ Continued e-Survey questions and rounding with operating staff as part of the patient safety program every two years

As a result of these actions and improvements, agreement with the statement "The Safe Surgery Saves Lives (SSSL) process took place as well as you would like if you or a family member were the patient" (which was already 88% in 2009) has increased to almost 100% (Figure 4.24).

In addition to the surgical care safety improvements described previously, the Human Factors Department has also taken several actions to improve patient safety during surgical care. For example, human factors engineers and frontline OR staff developed a process and OR Passport form to overcome barriers when identifying patients in the OR setting and labeling specimens, transfusing blood, and performing other high-risk interventions (Figure 4.25).

The nurse attaches the patient label to the OR passport at the time of the preoperative interview and utilizes the passport checklist to complete

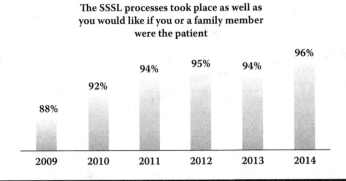

The SSSL processes took place as well as you would like if you or a family member were the patient

88%	92%	94%	95%	94%	96%
2009	2010	2011	2012	2013	2014

Figure 4.24   Agreement with the statement "The Safe Surgery Saves Lives (SSSL) process took place as well as you would like if you or a family member were the patient."

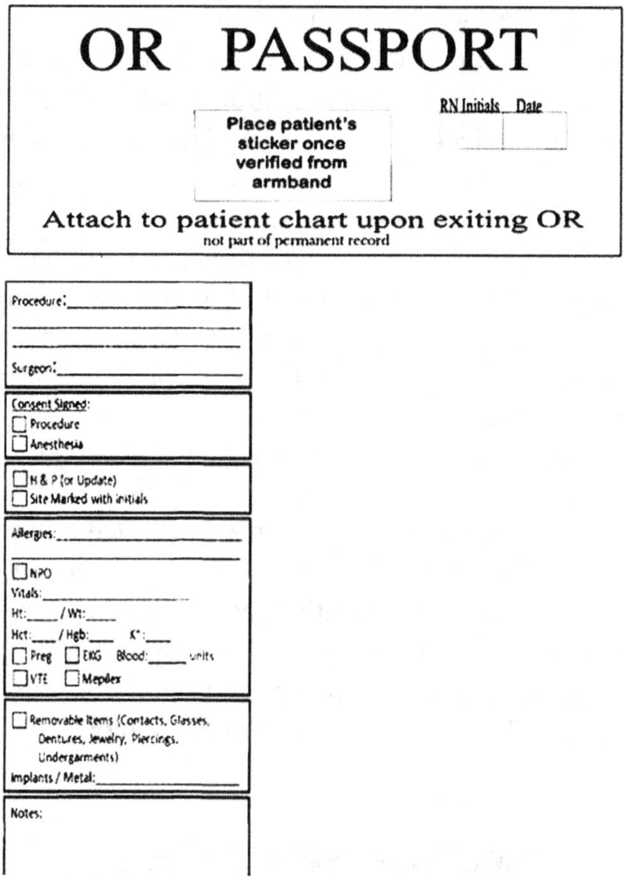

OR PASSPORT

RN Initials   Date

Place patient's
sticker once
verified from
armband

Attach to patient chart upon exiting OR
not part of permanent record

Procedure:_____

_____

_____

Surgeon:_____

Consent Signed:
☐ Procedure
☐ Anesthesia

☐ H & P (or Update)
☐ Site Marked with initials

Allergies:_____

☐ NPO
Vitals:_____
Ht:____ / Wt:____
Hct:____ / Hgb:____   K⁺:____
☐ Preg ☐ EKG Blood:____ units
☐ VTE ☐ Mepdex

☐ Removable Items (Contacts, Glasses,
    Dentures, Jewelry, Piercings,
    Undergarments)
Implants / Metal:_____

Notes:

Figure 4.25   OR passport.

the interview. When the patient arrives in the OR suite, the nurse initials and dates the passport as a second confirmation of patient identification at sign-in.

REDI (Role Model, Engage, Direct, Inform) Surgeon

Although the SSSL checklist is a crucial component of ensuring the highest levels of patient safety during surgical care, the checklist and timeout process also need to support a culture of patient safety.

An approach to improving surgical practice at several hospitals within BHCS (before the merger) was developed with human factors to create a safer surgical team environment. There was also collaborative work with Kaiser Permanente, which shared its previous work to address technical and cultural aspects of safety through a formal team briefing process.

How can we enhance the current timeout process in a fast-paced environment to promote a culture of safety through leadership and engagement of staff? Checklists are useful but are not sufficient to eliminate surgical error, and a key for the effective use of a checklist is to establish a cohesive team. Based on human factors science and working with collaborators, four key leadership techniques have been identified for enhancing teamwork, communication, and safety in a procedure-driven environment. The REDI (role model, engage, direct, inform) model of leadership (Figure 4.26) establishes a positive team climate. These techniques require practice to achieve the desired outcome of all members of the team being key to patient outcomes and a culture of safety.

Here are four important leadership techniques for the surgeon:

■ First, form a team. Before the procedure, introduce and establish a communicative interaction with each team member. Greet each team member by name and establish a positive tone.
■ Next, "humanize" the patient. Describe the patient as "Mrs. Johnson, a retired elementary teacher who really hopes that this knee surgery allows her to be able to be more active and enjoy her time with her

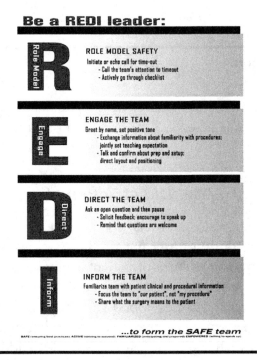

Figure 4.26 Be a REDI leader.

grandchildren" (rather than just "my second total knee replacement"). Your team members will be more likely to speak up or double check an important item for Mrs. Johnson than a "nonhuman total knee number 2."

■ Champion the timeout process to role-model patient safety. Set the standard. Stop what you are doing, focus on the timeout process and actively participate. The OR team members will follow your lead to see the importance and value of safety during the procedure.

■ Finally, and possibly most important, actively empower the entire team to communicate concerns. It is so much better to graciously thank a team member for voicing a concern than to ask, "Why didn't you say something?" after an adverse outcome. This requires an active request for input, not just a willingness to listen.

These techniques were judged as very important to both surgeons and OR staff in a survey (Table 4.1). The two groups were closely aligned, except for "engaging the team," where the surgeon perception was very important as compared with the nurse perception. The same survey also demonstrated that these techniques were not routinely used. With collaborators, we developed a training program to help surgeons learn these techniques.

Table 4.1   Survey Results: Importance of Surgeon Leadership Behaviors

Surgeon Behavior	Respondents	"Very Important" for Patient Care	"Somewhat Important" for Patient Care	"Not at All Important" for Patient Care	χ^2 Probability
Engage the team	Surgeons	70%	30%	1%	0.00
	OR staff	44%	48%	8%	
Introduce the patient	Surgeons	73%	24%	2%	0.35
	OR staff	74°%	26%	0%	
Set safety focus	Surgeons	82%	14%	4%	0.67
	OR staff	82%	16%	2%	
Empower the team	Surgeons	76%	21%	2%	0.99
	OR staff	76%	22%	2%	

Pharmacy Care

Improving Medication Safety

In a recent BSWH initiative to improve care for elderly patients who are discharged from the hospital, a multidisciplinary team that included a pharmacist, an advanced practice nurse, and a social worker helped to facilitate elderly patients' transition from hospital to home. In one case, the social worker visited the patient's home and found that the patient had over thirty prescription medications, including several duplicate medications, and that the patient had inadvertently mixed her dog's medications with her own medications. The social worker notified the pharmacist, who went to the patient's house, called the patient's primary care physician, and organized all the medications in one afternoon. Pharmacists play a crucial role as part of the health care team, and efforts to improve medication safety are important to everyone who wants to ensure safer patient care.

Medication safety is a key component of patient safety. Medication errors are a common cause of preventable adverse events both in and out of the hospital, causing the IoM to call for health care delivery organizations to establish system-oriented approaches to medication error reduction (Institute for Healthcare Improvement, *Conduct Patient Safety Leadership WalkRounds*™).

While medication safety has always been an important part of the BSWH patient safety culture, the organization formally committed to an organization-wide strategy to reduce medication errors in 2005, when the Board of Trustees adopted the six interventions of the IHI 100,000 Lives Campaign, one of which was to prevent adverse drug events by implementing medication reconciliation (Chapter 1). Since then, the organization has implemented a variety of initiatives focused on preventing medication errors.

In 2010, with increased focus on patient safety related to medications and medication reconciliation from regulatory/compliance as well as an internal desire to have dedicated resources for this important work, BHCS hired a director-level pharmacist to oversee medication safety. This is still a key role in helping to proactively identify medications risks as well as championing medication related initiatives across BSWH. This individual is a member of the BSWH Patient Safety Committee and participates in patient safety site visits related to the Patient Safety Assessment Program. Below are some key initiatives that the medication safety director has been involved with.

Medication safety initiatives include:

■ Medication reconciliation
■ Standardized medication error reports and adverse medication reaction reports across the system
  – Resulted in change in administration of Vancomycin based on data
■ Institute for Safe Medication Practices (ISMP) Initiatives
  – Implement Tallman lettering in the EHR
  – Do Not Crush List
  – ISMP Targeted Medication Safety Best Practices
    • All Vinca alkaloids dispensed in IV mini-bag to prevent inadvertent intrathecal administration
    • Computer systems changed to default to weekly dosing for oral methotrexate
    • Removal of glacial acetic acid
    • Utilization of metric units for patient weights (in process, barriers of current scales with both units, as well as software configurations that allow for both pounds/kilograms)
    • Oral liquid measuring devices (in process, trying to also align to same manufacturer for ENFit syringes as well)
    • Pharmacy preparation/dispensing of non-unit dose oral liquids (in process, the number of medications continues to be reduced, which are not supplied by pharmacy in patient specific unit doses. Focusing on high-risk medications/patient populations first)
  – National Alert Network—phenylephrine/ephedrine
    • Addressed purchasing practices to ensure better differentiation between these two products
■ IV Pump Library Continuous Quality Improvement
  – Adjustment of limits to decrease nuisance alerts
  – Changes to enhance usability and increase library compliance
■ Insulin U-500
  – Standardized policy and practices
■ Sentinel event alert follow-up
  – #52: Safe Injection Practices Policy
  – #54: Safe Use of Health Information Technology—established accountability for ongoing testing of medication-related functionality in all identified software applications.

- Standardized lipid rescue kit (contents with instructions)
- Formation of a Pharmacy Medication Safety Team (meets monthly to identify and discuss medication safety concerns)
  - Formally reviews ISMP Quarterly Action Agendas
    - Reduced stocked quantities of levothyroxine 25 µg tablets stocked in automated dispensing cabinets to prevent potential of 10-fold dosing error
    - Ferumoxytol injection—administration and monitoring practices implemented
- Zolpidem
  - Limited dose on order set to 5 mg for all patients
  - Removed default PRN ordering on order sets
- Standard concentrations
- Insulin
  - Insulin pen devices dispensed directly from pharmacy to ensure appropriate labeling, including tamper evident seal
  - Beyond-use dating applied by pharmacy before dispensing
  - Standardized labeling methodology
- Semirigid sterile water bottles use for cardiopulmonary (instead of bag)
- Crash cart standardization

Medication Reconciliation

A pharmacy technician at one BSWH facility was able to help the pharmacist retime the dose of a blood thinner when a patient was noted to have accidentally taken an evening dose the morning prior to arriving in the emergency department. The technician clarified with the patient and informed the pharmacist that the order needed to be retimed to the next day.

Medication reconciliation is the process of comparing the medication information the patient brought to the hospital with the medication ordered for the patient by the hospital, by a qualified individual, to identify and resolve medication discrepancies. This process should ensure accurate and consistent communication of a patient's medication information through all transitions of care where new medications are ordered or existing medication orders are continued. Medication reconciliation improves patient safety by:

- Standardizing and improving workflow for the medication reconciliation process
- Reducing duplications, omissions, and inaccurate data
- Enabling patients to be provided with a more complete and accurate list of medication instructions at discharge
- Improving provider satisfaction

Medication reconciliation is a very challenging and complex process that remains a significant patient safety concern. It can impact patients at any transition point during their care. BSWH proactively works to enhance medication reconciliation by utilizing improvement strategies and tactics to improve this process. This section highlights some of the ongoing work that the Medication Reconciliation Steering Committee and Subgroups (Figure 4.27) lead.

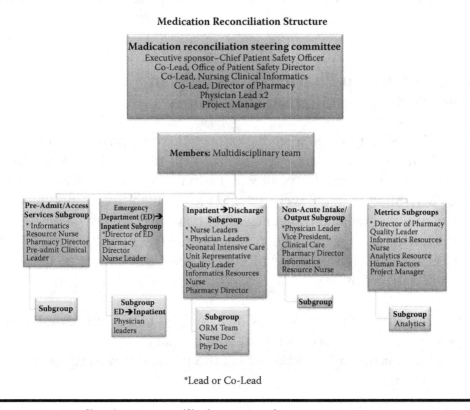

Figure 4.27   Medication Reconciliation Committee structure.

The Medication Reconciliation Steering Committee meets every two weeks to review enhancements to the medication reconciliation process, develop and update policies and procedures, provide direction to IS medication reconciliation groups, and oversee updates in the EHR.

Medication Reconciliation Committee Subgroups include the Pre-Admit/Access Services group, ED to Inpatient group, Inpatient to Discharge group, Nonacute/Outpatient group, and Metrics group. Subgroups commit to meet regularly and actively participate in the process of identifying key stakeholders from clinical areas who can detail the current state of medication reconciliation and help to identify barriers and solutions. Examples of subgroup activities include the following:

■ Map out workflow to determine suboptimal processes that consume resources and result in a potentially inaccurate patient medication list
■ Identify barriers using a "fishbone diagram"
■ Define metrics and create an enterprise report

An example of the workflow for one area (outpatient/inpatient integrated discharge medication reconciliation) is presented in Figure 4.28.

Emergency Room Pharmacy Technician Medication Reconciliation Pilot Study

One BSWH hospital piloted a study that included two pharmacy technicians working seven days on and seven days off in the ED. They worked from 1:30 pm until midnight (peak volume in the ED). From March 1, 2014, through May 31, 2014, there were 1090 ED-to-inpatient medication reconciliations, with 8018 mediations reconciled. The average time to complete the outpatient medication reconciliation was 13 minutes. Benefits created by the utilization of these pharmacy technicians for medication reconciliation in the ED included the following:

■ Use of a focused group of individuals trained to a standardized, enterprise process to reduce variability in data entry
■ Enhanced clarity about who "owns" the process of medication reconciliation

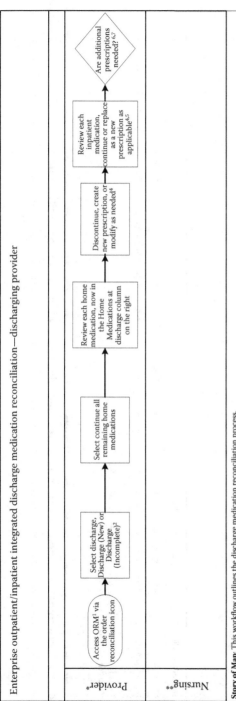

Enterprise outpatient/inpatient integrated discharge medication reconciliation—discharging provider

Provider*

- Access ORM[1] via the order reconciliation icon
- Select discharge, Discharge (New) or Discharge (Incomplete)[2]
- Select continue all remaining home medications
- Review each home medication, now in the Home Medications at discharge column on the right
- Discontinue, create new prescription, or modify as needed[4]
- Review each inpatient medication, continue or replace as a new prescription as applicable[4,5]
- Are additional prescriptions needed? [6,7]

Nursing**

Story of Map: This workflow outlines the discharge medication reconciliation process.

1 ORM = Order reconciliation manager. Note areas excluded from the ORM requirement include outpatient laboratory and outpatient imaging.
2 If a consulting provider entered scripts into discharge ORM before the primary provider began discharge, the consultant would save as incomplete. Refer to the consultant workflow for more information.
4 Use inline action button, right-click, or use drop-down arrow to perform these actions.
5 If there are inpatient medications with incomplete information, the medication or prescription modification screen displays if continued. If replace with New Home medication or replace with New Prescription is selected, additional forms of the medication will display to choose from if available. Alternatively, you can select other medications and replace the home medication or inpatient medication with a new prescription.
6 Schedule II medications should be entered via Enter Prescriptions icon addition to hand writing on official schedule II prescription form to maintain the patient's medication history and for the patient to have an accurate discharge medication list.
7 Surgeons/proceduralists sometimes give prescriptions ahead of time for scheduled outpatient surgeries/procedures so the patient or patient's representative can have them ready at home post discharge. These should be entered as a "save only" (unless the home medication has been entered previously as a home medication).

Note steps 6 and 7 are necessary to maintain the patient's medication history and for the patient to have an accurate discharge medication list. The prescription will be saved rather than printed. Sort by Therapeutic category, select expand medications and show matching medications format layout—this is a one time display format setup.

* Provider refers to physicians, advanced practitioners, residents, fellows.
** Nursing refers to RN, LVN, Nursing Student.

Activities in gray are performed in the EHR.

Figure 4.28 Example of outpatient/inpatient discharge medication reconciliation. *(Continued)*

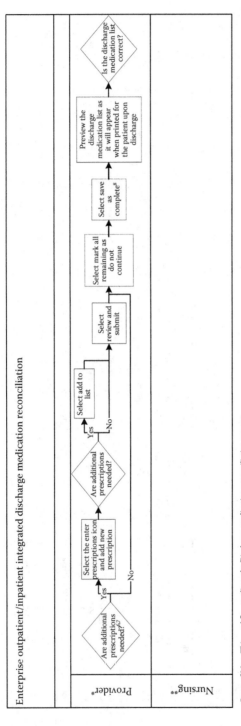

Enterprise outpatient/inpatient integrated discharge medication reconciliation

Story of Map: This workflow outlines the Discharge medication reconciliation process.

6 Schedule II medications should be entered via Enter Prescriptions icon in addition to hand writing on official schedule II prescription form to maintain the patient's medication history and for the patient to have an accurate discharge medication list.

7 Surgeons/proceduralists sometimes give prescriptions ahead of time for schedule outpatient surgeries/procedures so the patient or patients's representative can have them ready at home post discharge.

8 Refer to consultant workflow for save as complete vs. save incomplete.

* Provider refers to Physicians, advanced practitioners, residents, fellows.
** Nursing refers to RN, LVN, Nursing student.

Activities in gray are performed in the EHR.

Figure 4.28 (Continued)   Example of outpatient/inpatient discharge medication reconciliation.   (Continued)

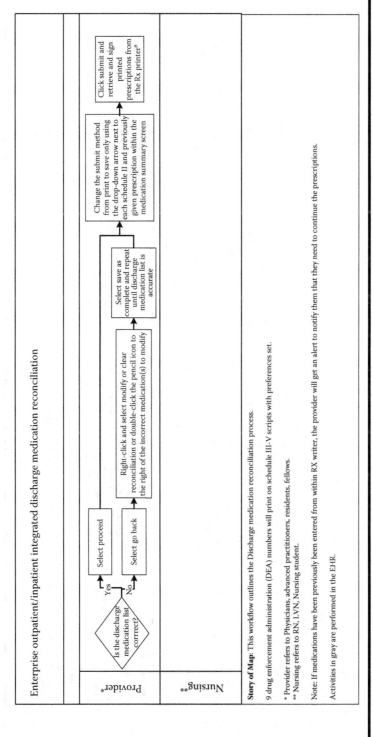

Enterprise outpatient/inpatient integrated discharge medication reconciliation

Provider*

Nursing**

Select proceed

Is the discharge medication list correct?

Yes

No

Select go back

Right-click and select modify or clear reconciliation or double-click the pencil icon to the right of the incorrect medication(s) to modify

Select save as complete and repeat until discharge medication list is accurate

Change the submit method from print to save only using the drop-down arrow next to each schedule II and previously given prescription within the medication summary screen

Click submit and retrieve and sign printed prescriptions from the Rx printer[9]

Story of Map: This workflow outlines the Discharge medication reconciliation process.

9 drug enforcement administration (DEA) numbers will print on schedule III-V scripts with preferences set.

* Provider refers to Physicians, advanced practitioners, residents, fellows.
** Nursing refers to RN, LVN, Nursing student.

Note: If medications have been previously been entered from within RX writer, the provider will get an alert to notify them that they need to continue the prescriptions.

Activities in gray are performed in the EHR.

Figure 4.28 (Continued) Example of outpatient/inpatient discharge medication reconciliation.   *(Continued)*

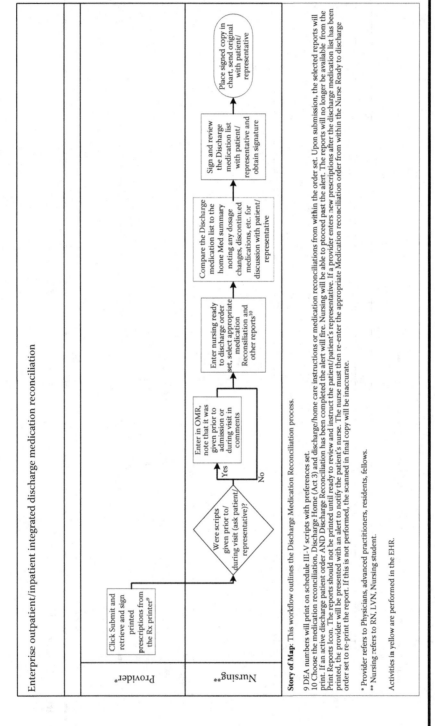

Enterprise outpatient/inpatient integrated discharge medication reconciliation

Provider*

Click Submit and retrieve and sign printed prescriptions from the Rx printer[9]

Were scripts given prior to/during visit (ask patient/representative)?

Yes → Enter in OMR, note that it was given prior to admission or during visit in comments

No

Nursing*

Enter nursing ready to discharge order set, select appropriate medication Reconsiliation and other reports[10]

Compare the Discharge medication list to the home Med summary noting any dosage changes, discontinued medications, etc. for discussion with patient/representative

Sign and review the Discharge medication list with patient/representative and obtain signature

Place signed copy in chart, send original with patient/representative

Story of Map: This workflow outlines the Discharge Medication Reconciliation process.

9 DEA numbers will print on schedule III-V scripts with preferences set.
10 Choose the medication reconciliation, Discharge Home (Act 3) and discharge/home care instructions or medication reconciliations from within the order set. Upon submission, the selected reports will print. If an active discharge patient order AND Discharge Reconciliation has been completed the alert will fire. Nursing will be able to proceed past the alert. The reports will no longer be available from the Print Reports Icon. The reports should not be printed until ready to review and instruct the patient/patient's representative. If a provider enters new prescriptions after the discharge medication list has been printed, the provider will be presented with an alert to notify the patient's nurse. The nurse must then re-enter the appropriate Medication reconciliation order from within the Nurse Ready to discharge order set to re-print the report. If this is not performed, the scanned in final copy will be inaccurate.

* Provider refers to Physicians, advanced practitioners, residents, fellows.
** Nursing refers to RN, LVN, Nursing student.

Activities in yellow are performed in the EHR.

Figure 4.28 (Continued)   Example of outpatient/inpatient discharge medication reconciliation.

- Reduction of the burden on nurses and physicians to obtain and verify a patient's home medication list in an efficient manner
- Enhanced cost effectiveness from designating pharmacy technicians (rather than nurses physicians) as responsible for verifying the accuracy of the medication record

To be successful in their role, pharmacy technicians need to be familiar with common medications, dosages, and frequencies to ensure that an accurate picture of a patient's home medications can be constructed, especially when the patient or transferring facility provides little or no home medication information. This knowledge gives pharmacy technicians the ability to thoroughly review home medication lists with patients, family members, and caregivers. To do this, they may utilize the Facts and Comparisons website or BSWH resources to display pictures of medications, dosage standards, and other information. They may also contact outpatient pharmacies as well as the patient's primary care provider for detailed prescription information. When not focusing on these tasks, pharmacy technicians may carry out other job duties, such as auditing charts or compounding medications for inpatient units.

Conclusion

The fourth phase of the journey to safer patient care is focused on developing, implementing, and sustaining specific processes that drive patient safety. Examples of such processes include mortality reduction initiatives; tools to improve communication; patient safety huddles; strategies to engage patients and families in the patient safety program; and initiatives focused on specific service lines such as ambulatory care, cardiovascular care, and surgical care. These processes support and drive an organizational culture of patient safety and lay the groundwork for the next phase of the patient safety journey, which will leverage technology to enhance patient safety and facilitate the delivery of STEEEP care.

Chapter 5

Leveraging Technology

The journey to safer patient care starts with the building of a strong foundation for a patient safety program, the creation of a culture of patient safety, the integration of that culture, and the building of specific processes of care to drive patient safety. The final step in the journey involves the leveraging of technology to assimilate patient safety data, measure and report the outcomes of patient safety initiatives, and improve communication and information exchange among care providers. Specific uses of technology to drive patient safety include tools to measure and analyze adverse events (AEs), department-specific patient safety programs in nonclinical areas, EHRs to standardize safety processes, gaming technology to improve physician–nurse communication, and a data mining laboratory (DML) to provide a data-rich environment to assist with identifying and analyzing patient data to help drive improvement (see Figure 5.1).

Baylor Adverse Event Measurement Tool

In 2006, IHI began encouraging health care providers to implement the Global Trigger Tool (GTT) to determine and monitor patient all-cause harm (Institute for Healthcare Improvement, *IHI Global Trigger Tool for Measuring Adverse Events*). The use of "triggers," or clues, to identify AEs enables measurement of the overall level of patient harm in a health care delivery organization. Those trained in the methodology conduct retrospective reviews of patient records

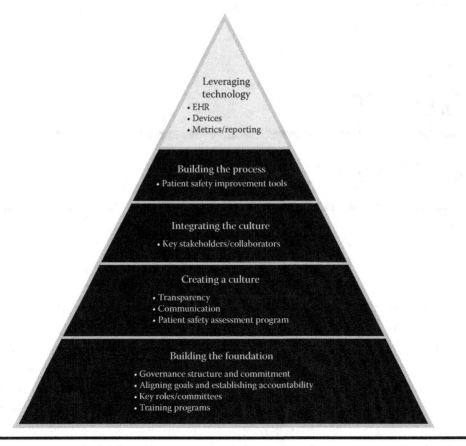

Figure 5.1   Patient safety framework for achieving safe health care. EHR, electronic health record.

using triggers to identify possible AEs. These data provide important information on the following:

- AEs per 1000 patient days
- AEs per 100 admissions
- Percentage of admissions with an AE

Unlike voluntary reporting systems, which underestimate the true rate of AEs (Samore et al. 2004), trigger tools such as the GTT rely on objective clinical records, rather than voluntary reports by clinical staff and hospital employees who might fear disciplinary consequences of reporting AEs.

To expand and make more actionable the AE data collected by the GTT, BSWH developed the Baylor AE Measurement Tool (BAEMT; Figure 5.2).

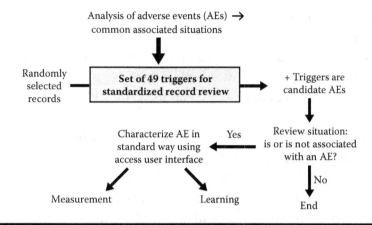

Figure 5.2   BAEMT: overview of trigger tool method.

The BAEMT measures the overall incidence of AEs as well as critical information such as the following:

- AE preventability
- Presence of AE on admission
- Relation of AE to care provided or not provided
- Narrative descriptions

An initial study of the BAEMT found that in 2008, 91% of identified AEs were in patients with lengths of stay (LOS) of three days or more; there were 6.4 AEs per 100 discharges with LOS of less than three days vs. 27.1 AEs per 100 discharges with LOS of three days or greater. Over four years, 16,172 medical records were reviewed; 14,184 had positive triggers, 17.1% of which were associated with an AE. Most AEs were identified via the "surgical" (36.3%) and "patient care" (36.0%) trigger modules. Reviewers showed fair to good agreement ($\kappa = 0.62$), and hospital clinical leaders strongly agreed that the identified events were AEs. Overall, the study showed that the GTT could be adapted to health care organizations' goals and limited resources (Kennerly et al. 2013).

In a second study of the BAEMT, patient records were examined from monthly random samples of adults admitted to eight acute care hospitals from 2007 to 2011 with LOS ≥3 days. Overall AE incidence was measured, as well as AEs that were present on admission, AE severity, whether the AE resulted from care provided vs. care omitted, AE preventability, and patient harm category. Overlap with commonly used AE-detection systems was also measured. In this study, professional nurse reviewers abstracted 9017 records, recording triggers, and AEs. Medical record/account numbers were matched to identify overlapping voluntary reports or AHRQ PSIs.

The BAEMT expands on knowledge about AEs gained by patient safety administrative data-based measures (such as AHRQ PSIs) and

- Provides hospitals with facility-specific data showing rates and types of AEs associated with measurable patient harm through randomly chosen chart reviews (~2%)
- Enables health care delivery systems to apply resources toward reducing patient harm through prioritization of concerns and implementation of process improvements that will provide the greatest benefit to patient safety
- Allows for data analysis and trending to target when and where intervention may be needed to address AEs

Patient Safety in Information Services

As part of the IS Department's enhanced focus on patient safety, when a new process is rolled out, a proactive risk assessment is conducted to see whether the plan could impact patient care or patient safety. For example, if there is a planned upgrade to the EHR, IS staff use a checklist to predict what could go wrong with the upgrade and how to prevent these potential problems. In one case, IS used a failure mode effects analysis to determine that the department needed to obtain additional support for physicians before a planned EHR upgrade could occur. The upgrade was postponed while this support was obtained, and the upgrade was subsequently rolled out effectively. Patient safety is a top priority for all staff and all departments, whether or not they are involved in direct patient care, and is the most important consideration when new processes or technology are introduced into the organization.

The journey toward safer patient care depends on the establishment of an organizational culture of patient safety (Chapter 2). To ensure that this culture exists across the entire organization, rather than just on the frontline and in clinical areas, nonclinical departments may need to establish their own patient safety program. For example, the BSWH IS department and Office of Patient Safety implemented a patient safety program in Fall 2013 in recognition of the key role played by health information technology (HIT) in facilitating safe patient care (Corrigan et al. 2001). Further validating the need for an enhanced culture of safety in IS were the ongoing challenges that IT was facing with the implementation of the EHR and other systems. The ability for the clinical and IS teams to partner and resolve patient safety concerns was essential. The IS patient safety program, which is led by a vice president-level executive sponsor and a team of champion volunteers, is based on the following framework:

■ The role that HIT plays in improving the quality, safety, and cost-effectiveness of care, as well as the patient's experience of care, should be recognized and supported.
■ Shared responsibility for patient safety must involve the entire health care team.
■ Processes, systems, and standards should be risk based and flexible and should promote patient safety and strong outcomes.
■ Reporting of patient safety events related to HIT is essential; a nonpunitive environment should be established to encourage reporting, learning, and improving.

The IS patient safety program initially aimed to spread patient safety awareness across the department with a variety of tactics and strategies with support from the Office of Patient Safety:

■ Promote the patient safety program in the new employee department orientation
■ Recognize outstanding patient safety work by staff
■ Create a version of the APPSS for IS staff
■ Share patient safety survey results with staff and develop action plans for improvement
■ Initiate a clinical observation program for IS staff to understand clinical workflows and processes
■ Include testimonials, speakers, and other patient safety presentations in employee meetings

- Publish patient safety topics via the intranet, departmental newsletters, and communication boards
- Utilize electronic display boards to connect the clinical and IS environments (e.g., daily reports of admission, number of babies born)
- Create a nonpunitive environment where employees are empowered to raise issues and assist in their resolution
- Conduct joint RCA/case reviews with IS and clinical staff and provide summary of follow-up actions to address processes
- Provide feedback to staff and summarize actions taken to address processes
- As part of the CDAT Committee oversight, RCAs are conducted for EHR unplanned downtimes and extended planned downtimes
- Representatives from Nursing Informatics, Information Systems, Human Factors, Patient Safety, Pharmacy, and CDAT members, as well as physicians and other key stakeholders, make up this group
- The focus is to identify breakdown of processes and improvement strategies
- A detailed summary of the event is created with a timeline, root causes, and follow-up actions, and a log is kept with key information from these summaries to share with the CDAT Committee and leaders (Table 5.1)

To address the measurement of the patient safety culture, IS uses a modified version of the APPSS (Chapter 2). The Office of Patient Safety met with executive leaders from IS to gather support for rolling out an IS-specific patient safety survey. This survey asks respondents to indicate the degree to which they agree to statements that relate to the IS impact on patient safety and culture, including the following:

- Real-time recognition and reporting of technology risks are encouraged and valued.
- If I saw something being built or a process that could negatively impact patient safety, I would speak up.
- If my concerns are not adequately addressed, I will elevate my concern to protect the safety of the patient.
- It is an important priority of information technology to support direct patient care providers.
- The quality of work is not compromised to meet deadlines.

Table 5.1　Example of Root Cause Analysis Log

Date of Incident	Time	Owner (Vice President)	Duration (HH:MM)	Impacted IS Service(s)	Business Impact		Root Cause		Ticket Number
					Type	Description	Type	Description	

- My department receives feedback about how our work affects patient safety events such as documentation errors, medication errors, and other errors or risks.
- I have seen positive changes in practice as a result of reporting errors and risks.
- In my department, the staffing is adequate to promote safe, consistent support for day-to-day operations.
- The "Stop the Line" policy makes me feel more confident about speaking up to protect the safety of the patient.

The IS patient safety survey also allows respondents to write comments, including both positive feedback and suggested opportunities for improvement.

As a result of the first two years of survey data, IS further developed several planned initiatives to illustrate to employees the connection between patient safety and IS, and reinforce the accountability all organizational members have for ensuring the highest levels of patient care. Examples of these plans include the following:

- Employees from IS will visit clinical areas to see how IS applications and downtimes impact patient care and patient safety.
- IS is developing a tool to enable employees to report concerns anonymously.
- IS is launching a program to acknowledge and recognize employees mentioned by survey respondents for their exemplary behavior in patient safety.

One IS executive speaks to the impact of IS processes on patient safety: "When someone mentions patient safety, people tend to think about the need to prevent big clinical AEs. We are trying to close the gap on everything that could go wrong when there is a system outage. For example, an outage of the system could cause medication delays. And then there would be patients who would be in pain because of an EHR outage. This is why we are striving for zero downtime." The IS patient safety survey has helped employees to see the connection between their jobs and patient safety, even if they do not work on the frontlines of clinical care.

Electronic Health Record

Technology can enable the standardization of processes that clinicians need to follow to keep patients safe. For example, clinical leaders at BSWH created a nurse-driven protocol to prevent catheter-associated urinary tract infections. The protocol defines guidelines for the length of time a catheter should be kept in. After the medical executive committees approved the protocol, BSWH clinical informatics leaders analyzed the organization's order sets and identified all the processes for which physicians might order catheters. Different variations of an order were merged into one single order that describes all the approved indications for the catheter.

The system tracks how long the catheter has been in so that the tracking process is not subject to human error and has eliminated a non-direct care activity for nursing. Before the launch of EHRs, someone on the unit would go to every nurse, every day, and ask, "Does the patient have a catheter? When was it put in?" Nurses had to keep track of this information in a manual spreadsheet. Now, the process is automated. An example of the midwelling catheter assessment as it appears in an EHR screen shot is presented in Figure 5.3. The nurse receives an alert from the EHR when the indication is no longer valid and it is time to consider removing the catheter.

Lines/Tubes/Drains	<All>					
Show Inactive	Airway, Central Lines, Gastrointestinal Tube, GU Tubes, Intraosseous, Other Infusion, … ▾					
Observation	Site		Start Date	End Date	Days Since Insertion	Status
▾ **Central Lines**						
Pulmonary Artery Catheter Asse...	Insert: 08/20/2015 Site: #1 right internal jugular vein base thermodilution catheter		8/20/2015 5:19:00 PM		1	Active
Central Line Assessment	Insert: 08/20/2015 Site: #1 right internal jugular vein double lumen introducer		8/20/2015 5:13:00 PM		1	Active
Central Line Assessment	Insert: 08/20/2015 Site: #2 left subclavian vein triple lumen central venous catheter		8/20/2015 5:14:00 PM		1	Active
▾ **GU Tubes**						
Indwelling Catheter Assessment	Insert: 08/20/2015 Site: #1 indwelling urethral catheter, 16 Fr. double lumen		8/20/2015 5:20:00 PM		1	Active
▾ **Peripheral Lines**						
Arterial Line Assessment	Insert: 08/20/2015 Site: #1 right brachial artery		8/20/2015 5:15:00 PM		1	Active
Peripheral Vascular Access Asses...	Insert: 08/20/2015 Site: #1 left lower arm 20 gauge		8/20/2015 11:25:00 AM		1	Active
▾ **Tubes**						
Chest Tube Assessment	Insert: 08/20/2015 Site: #1 chest tube midline, mediastinal		8/20/2015 5:35:00 PM		1	Active

Figure 5.3   Lines, tubes, and drains.

The ongoing development of an HIT infrastructure has enormous potential to reduce medical errors and improve patient safety (Corrigan et al. 2001), prompting numerous government and nonprofit entities to call for the widespread adoption and implementation of EHRs (Agency for Healthcare Research and Quality, *Electronic Health Records*; Centers for Medicare and Medicaid Services, *The Official Web Site for the Medicare and Medicaid Electronic Health Records (EHR) Incentive Programs*; HealthIT.gov; Institute of Medicine 2004). Currently, the meaningful use of EHRs is a prerequisite for eligible professionals and hospitals to qualify for CMS Incentive Programs, with "meaningful use" defined as the use of certified EHR technology to

■ Improve quality, safety, and efficiency and reduce health disparities
■ Engage patients and families
■ Improve care coordination, population health, and public health
■ Maintain privacy and security of patient health information (HealthIT .gov)

EHRs improve patient safety through enhanced standardization of care processes, real-time clinical decision support and feedback, more efficient clinical workflow, reduction in medical errors, and more reliable documentation of care processes and outcomes.

Leadership and Governance

To ensure that EHRs drive improved patient safety, health care organizations must include patient safety leaders in governance processes surrounding HIT and information systems improvement. At BSWH, all EHR changes need to be approved by a committee (named "Workgroup 1") comprising clinical leaders as well as experts from the IT, Patient Safety, Clinical Informatics, and Human Factors departments. This committee aims to standardize care through the organization's EHR and ensure that the EHR yields streamlined workflows that support practice standards and reliable data and facilitates documentation that is less subject to human error than paper-based records. For example, when U.S. health care delivery organizations first began to adopt EHRs, clinical practice leaders in coordination with nurses and other clinicians were sometimes required to document care processes and events (e.g., patient falls) in multiple places in EHRs. Workgroup 1 develops and implements policies to support the documentation of each process or event in a single location in the EHR. This helps to ensure that EHR reports are standardized, reliable, and useful in the analysis of the effects of targeted care process improvements.

In addition to its work developing and implementing EHR policies and improving EHR documentation and standardization, Workgroup 1 evaluates and tests all potential changes to the EHR through shadow charting, or end user testing. Shadow charting facilitates end user involvement in ongoing EHR development and ensures that the EHR is constantly dynamic and responsive to changes in the health care environment. In addition, shadow charting enables any potential issues or workflow gaps surrounding EHR changes to be identified and corrected before these changes go live.

Electronic Health Record End User Survey

Surveying EHR users about their experiences is important because their feedback can be used to guide improvement decisions and prioritize improvement activities. In 2013, BSWH developed a nurse, pharmacist, and physician user survey to measure feedback about its EHR. The survey allows the measurement of end-user feedback in a standardized manner so that trends in the data can be followed across facilities and over time.

To develop the BSWH survey tool, subject matter experts (SMEs) from across the organization undertook a literature review of other EHR surveys. Nine individual survey tools informed the initial BSWH list of survey items: four of the tools focused on physicians within a primary care setting (Hoonakker et al. 2010; Husch et al. 2005; Likourezos et al. 2004; Tannery et al. 2011); three focused on nurses (Graham et al. 2004; Nemeth et al. 2009; Rothschild et al. 2005); one had been created for a broad provider audience (nurses, physicians, midlevel providers) (Institute for Safe Medication Practices); and one was specific to the emergency department (Rosenstein and O'Daniel 2008). Potential survey items were drawn from these tools and were reviewed and modified by BSWH SMEs, including nurse and physician informatics leaders and experts in patient safety, human factors, informatics, survey design, and statistics.

Construct domains for the survey were developed based on previous research (Manojlovich and DeCicco 2007) and the input of BSWH informatics leaders. These domains are described in Table 5.2. A screen shot from the EHR survey is depicted in Figure 5.4.

Table 5.2 BSWH Electronic Health Record Survey Tool Domains

Training/ competency	The degree to which the end user has received education that has prepared her/him for use of the EHR, and the confidence the end user has using the EHR
Usability	The perceived ease of use of the EHR, including navigating, viewing, editing, and entering information
Usefulness	The degree to which the end user finds that the EHR enables (vs. interferes with) his/her daily work
Infrastructure	The end user perception of availability and quality of the EHR software/hardware when needed, including access, slowness, and automated log-offs
End user support	The degree to which the end user can be provided with solutions when she/he experiences problems with the EHR

Electronic Health Record (EHR) Survey

Thank you for taking the time to complete this survey. Your responses are very important and will be kept strictly anonymous.
Please allow about 5 - 10 minutes to complete the survey. It is complete only when you select the "Submit" button on the last page. Please do <u>not</u> forward this link to anyone. Thank you for your help.

Does your current job role require that you use the EHR/ Eclipsys?

○ Yes   ○ No

Do you normally work at least 2 shifts each week?

○ Yes   ○ No

Please rate each statement with the response that best describes your experience with the Electronic Health Record (EHR)/ Eclipsys. Please select N/A if the statement does not apply to you.

	Strongly Agree	Agree	Neutral	Disagree	Strongly Disagree	N/A
The training I received related to the EHR was effective.	○	○	○	○	○	○
I am confident using the EHR.	○	○	○	○	○	○
I am able to find where I need to document patient care.	○	○	○	○	○	○
In general, I am not concerned about making errors in documentation in the EHR.	○	○	○	○	○	○

Figure 5.4 EHR nursing survey.

Examples of specific survey items include the following:

- The content is laid out in an understandable way.
- In general, the screen display is easy to read.
- Documentation through the EHR has improved patient safety.
- The training I received related to the EHR was effective.
- The EHR provides useful alerts/reminders.
- I am able to find where I need to document patient care.
- I am confident using the EHR.

- Access to EHR information has increased patient safety.
- The EHR makes it easier to assume care for transferred patients.

The nurse survey was initially launched in 2011. Nurses were surveyed again in the summer of 2013 across eleven hospitals via online survey management software. Frontline nurses who engaged in direct patient interaction were included. Invitations for the online survey were delivered to participants' employer-based e-mail addresses and included a link to the survey tool. Participants were given two reminders and twenty-one business days to complete the survey. Interim response rate reports were provided to nursing administration at each facility to encourage participation.

Physicians were first surveyed in 2013. Physicians practicing within a hospital setting at five hospitals (one urban, four community hospitals) in the Dallas-Fort Worth metroplex were included. Links to anonymous surveys were sent from each hospital chief medical officer, and paper surveys were distributed during standing meetings (e.g., Town Hall, Tumor Board). Providers were asked to self-select their specialty and mode of EHR training (classroom, online, or both) and indicate their level of interest in further EHR training. Physicians were able to complete the survey online or via paper over a six-week period.

For each survey item, an opportunity index is calculated by finding the opportunity for improvement weighted by the item's association with overall satisfaction. This index helps organizational leaders to prioritize improvement activities by identifying those survey items that have a large opportunity for improvement and may make the most difference to users in terms of their overall satisfaction with the EHR.

Case Study: Improving Infusion Pump Safety

To prevent medication errors related to IV medication administration and the adverse drug events these errors can cause, BSWH deployed approximately 4000 smart pumps between December 2005 and February 2013, using the following methods (Figure 5.5):

- In January 2013, a multidisciplinary steering committee was formed to provide process improvement of IV pump compliance and utilization across the organization.
- The desired outcomes included improving drug library utilization, with an initial focus on addressing high-alert medications.

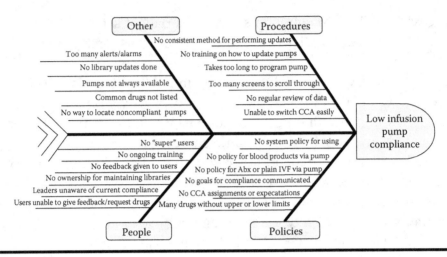

Figure 5.5 "Good Catches" with use of infusion pumps. Abx, antibiotics; CCA, clinical care area; IVF, intravenous fluids.

- An extensive review of the entire drug library and clinical care areas was performed on a quarterly basis.
- Leaders and users were kept informed with monthly dashboards. Nursing teamed up with the Biomed Department to locate pumps with out-of-date libraries and find pumps on "simple" delivery for just-in-time education. In addition, nurses worked with the Pharmacy Department to optimize and set limits for the drugs in the library.
- The Human Factors Department performed staff interviews and observations to identify barriers to pump utilization and also designed effective reports with frequency and utilization of drugs.
- Training and staff reeducation were conducted, and an intranet website was developed to provide resources and support to end users.

As a result of these improvements, system pump library utilization increased from 39% to 88% from January 2013 through June 2015 (Figure 5.6).

In addition to improving utilization, the changes listed previously resulted in a 273% increase in "good catches" in programming errors that were prevented from reaching the patient (Figure 5.7).

These results illustrate how improvements in the safety of IV infusion delivery are possible and require a multidisciplinary approach. Ongoing communication between users, engagement of senior leaders, and collaborative work among disciplines and departments (e.g., nursing, human factors, patient safety, hospital councils, pharmacy, biomed, physicians, vendors) are all critical to achieving high-compliance usage and sustaining long-term improvement.

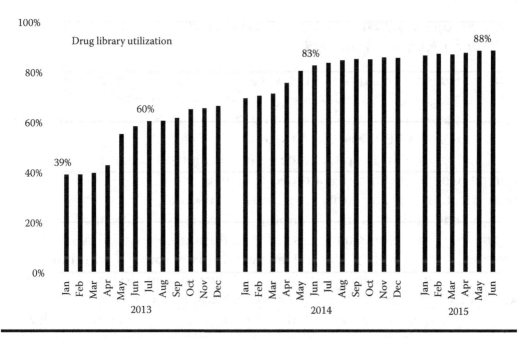

Figure 5.6   Monthly pump drug library utilization for the system, from January 2013 through June 2015.

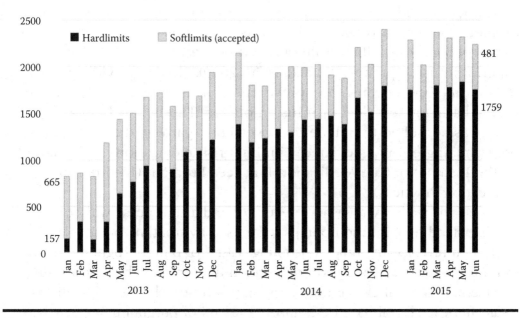

Figure 5.7   "Good catches" with use of the drug library on the infusion pumps. The numbers of hardlimits and accepted softlimits were the numbers of attempted doses that were flagged as outside safety limits by the drug library, and were corrected by the users.

Case Study: Improving Infusion Pump Safety: A Human Factors Approach

A more detailed version of the below case study focused on human factors (entitled "Engagement and Macroergonomics: Using Cognitive Engineering to Improve Patient Safety") appeared in the book *Cognitive Systems Engineering in Health Care* (CRC Press, 2014) (Xiao and Probst 2014).

Many patients in hospitals receive medications through infusion pumps, which can be programmed to deliver medications over a period with a set rate. Infusion pumps are used to deliver many high-risk, potent, and often life-sustaining medications to patients. Studies of adverse drug events have associated infusion medication with high error rates (Husch et al. 2005). However, infusion pumps with built-in safety mechanisms, such as dose error-reduction functions, otherwise known as "smart pumps," have not been shown to eliminate or even reduce adverse drug events (Rothschild et al. 2005). Dose error reduction functions are usually implemented through a "drug library," which is a list of medications with the possibility of including dose limits, default drug amounts, and default volumes. The drug library is a safety feature because dose errors outside limits may be flagged or stopped. A number of studies have illustrated defects in user interfaces that contributed to errors in programming infusion pumps (Graham et al. 2004). In one report, a usability evaluation did not result in the purchase of superior infusion pumps (Nemeth et al. 2009). Hospitals with smart pumps are seeking ways to improve safety, usually without the option of purchasing a new fleet of infusion pumps. The BSWH human factors team was consulted to initiate improvement regarding the reduction of programming errors associated with high-risk medications as identified by the Institute of Safe Medication Practices Program (Institute for Safe Medication Practices).

A field inspection with a nurse educator and a staff nurse was conducted to understand how infusion pumps were used by frontline nurses. The inspection revealed the time-consuming nature of pump programming. For example, to reach a life-support medication used frequently (vasopressin), a nurse had to scroll eleven times, with a response delay of 200 milliseconds after each scroll. From the start to the end of programming, it would take an experienced nurse over ninety seconds to complete such a task. A subsequent analysis of the composition of the drug library provided further evidence that opportunities for improvement were available to reduce programming errors that could reach patients and to reduce difficulties in programming smart pumps. The most important stakeholders were identified as the frontline nurses, who program smart pumps and "own" the responsibility of infusion medication safety. The human factors team identified a group of nurses and encouraged them to ask each other why the safety feature of programming the drug library that ensured that high-risk medications are administered at the appropriate clinical levels (e.g., volume and rate) was not used in programming the pumps. Examples were provided to the nurses to empower them to push beyond blaming individual nurse users. The barriers identified were surprisingly comprehensive and in line with findings in published reports. The nurses were then encouraged to present those findings to their peers as a list of "barriers" that impeded the use of the dose error-reduction system via the drug libraries (Figure 5.8).

The number of screen scrolls was calculated for the most frequently used medications to illustrate the need to reorganize the drug library. While this change was possible, the organization had not previously made the change because of a reliance on consensus and lack of understanding of human factors in listing many drug choices. The human factors team decided to invest time to develop an effective presentation on usability challenges such as the diagrammatic portraits of challenges in Figure 5.9. The leaders in the organization grasped the usability issue rapidly and overcame simplistic assumptions about the best ways to organize a drug library (such as alphabetical listing of all medications).

This case illustrates the large number of stakeholders that can be involved in any specific problem and the need to deploy methods of macroergonomics and cognitive engineering that take a comprehensive integrative systems approach. For example, expectations for compliant use of the drug libraries

Findings presented by ICU nurses

- Takes too long to program!
- Commonly used drugs are not easy to locate
  (e.g., Zosyn - piperacillin/tazobactam in medsurg, oncology and anti-infective CCAs)
- IVF/IVPB is not descriptive or intuitive for normal saline
- Unable to switch CCA libraries easily
- Not sure why most Abx/IVF are programmed
- Common doses are not included in CCA libraries
- Too many alerts (soft-limits)
- No organized ways to learn how to use the pumps exists

Figure 5.8   Findings presented by intensive care unit nurses.

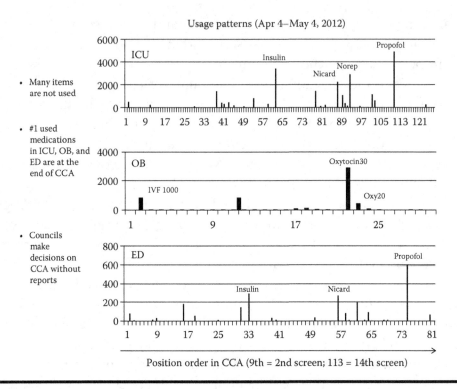

- Many items are not used

- #1 used medications in ICU, OB, and ED are at the end of CCA

- Councils make decisions on CCA without reports

Figure 5.9 Usability challenges. CCA, clinical care area; ED, emergency department; ICU, intensive care unit; OB, obstetrics.

during pump programming were set by administrative policies and guidelines. The skills necessary for programing infusion pumps, which were not intuitive, fell in the realm of professional nursing development. The service of pumps was provided by the biomedical engineering department. The pharmacy department held the responsibility for the drug library (with consultation and input from physicians and nurses). Routine reports on improvements to drug library usage, which were time consuming, were provided by the pump vendors and by an internal data analytics group.

Engaging stakeholders in the analysis process provided a number of benefits. In addition to improving the pump programming process itself, frontline clinicians and managers learned about programming errors framed on the axiom that human errors are inevitable and are to be expected and about the focus on minimizing patient harm as opposed to questioning their commitment to patient safety. A sample slide (Figure 5.10) was used for sharing the lessons learned in staff meetings. In addition to interviews and observations, cognitive engineering methods and concepts made essential contributions to safety improvements by providing visual representations to

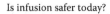

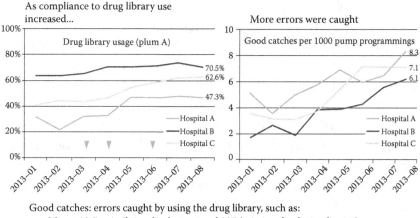

Is infusion safer today?

Good catches: errors caught by using the drug library, such as:
Meant 10.5 units/h insulin, but entered 105 (missing the decimal point)
Meant 1.8 units/h insulin, but entered 108 (pressing "0" instead of ".")
Meant 0.4 mcg/kg/h precedex, but entered 0.04 (entering an extra zero)

▼ 2013–03: super-usertrainings; 2013–04: drug library update; 2013–06: drug library
update

Figure 5.10   Lessons learned about infusion safety.

engage end users in designing reports to support frontline managers and
other key leaders to rapidly improve drug library compliance, in supporting reports to support drug library optimization, and in setting the systems
view of improvement. Cognitive engineering played a role in developing
the list of barriers and in the visual presentation of drug library usage logs.
By bringing new concepts and solutions to discussions with key stakeholders, the human factors team was able to motivate systematic approaches to
improve infusion safety.

Health care organizations can benefit significantly from cognitive engineering concepts and methods, especially if they are applied broadly
beyond simple device and interface design efforts and in conjunction with
other applicable methods. Assessment of policies, education strategy development, and cultural change initiatives are among the top areas where
cognitive engineering can lend methods and concepts about cognitive workload, expertise capturing, and performance support. To ensure a meaningful
impact on the quality of patient care, strategies that engage multiple stakeholders are essential. Some of the methods based on cognitive engineering
may be simplified and used by frontline clinicians, while others may be
used to generate materials that help frontline clinicians and managers gain
insight into cognitive work demands.

In the case of infusion pump medication safety improvement, it was clear early on that multiple stakeholders would be needed to contribute to the solution. It was productive to empower frontline users with rudimentary cognitive engineering concepts. This should serve as a reference for other health care organizations to use cognitive engineering methods to identify potential sources of barriers in using complex health technology. Hospital leaders and managers were shown usability challenges by visual portraits of the number of scrolls needed to program high-risk, time-critical medications. Cognitive engineering methods were useful to share insights and build a common ground for robust, effective improvement initiatives. Frontline nurses felt that their voices were heard when improvement in safety went beyond simply asking them to pay closer attention.

Gaming Technology for Physician–Nurse Communication

A young female nurse recently joined the medical-surgical staff at a national hospital and had never called a physician at night. After assessing a patient's status, she felt the situation warranted a call to the on-call consulting physician, whom she had never met before. The physician had worked at the hospital for several years. The nurse used a structured communication format (situation, background, assessment, and recommendation) but was abruptly interrupted by the physician, who requested an additional piece of information that the nurse did not have on hand. The physician lost his temper and spoke in an unprofessional manner to the nurse. The nurse blamed herself for the physician's reaction and is reluctant to call this or any other physician in the future regardless of perceived patient need.

Effective communication is the cornerstone of patient safety; leading organizations such as The Joint Commission and the IOM call for improved communication among health care team members (The Joint Commission, *National Patient Safety Goals;* Kohn et al. 1999). Ineffective interprofessional communication is a leading cause of preventable patient harm (Manojlovich and DeCicco 2007; Rosenstein and O'Daniel 2008). Despite the need for physicians and nurses to understand how professional, cultural, and personal differences can affect their communication, they usually receive limited training in communicating effectively with each other (Mannahan 2010).

Recently, BSWH-North collaborated with the University of Texas at Arlington and the University of Texas at Dallas to develop a gaming environment to improve communication skills between physicians and nurses who care for patients in acute care settings. The interactive game contains modules with virtual coaches to train and support communication practices. Specifically, the goals of the gaming project were to:

- Develop an interprofessional communication model for physician–nurse communication with both prescriptive components for targeted behaviors and descriptive components to simulate typical behaviors. The primary focus was communication about critical patient conditions between registered nurses and physicians on medical–surgical units.
- Develop a web-enabled serious game environment. The game, named "Communication Situation" (additional details are provided below), was designed as an integral content delivery component of an established training curriculum on interprofessional communication. An iterative process was used for game design with the participation of practicing nurses and physicians. Key features of the game include role-playing and adjustable communication styles.
- Evaluate the impact of a gaming environment approach to training on interprofessional communication practices, safety culture, and patient outcomes.

Communication Situation

The role-playing game "Communication Situation" allows health care professionals to explore communication styles and strategies and see themselves through the point of view of colleagues. The game provides complex and believable characters (nurses, physicians) with a variety of "personalities," or communication styles. To score well in the game, the player needs to adapt and strategize regarding ways to respond to the various communication styles encountered in a typical hospital setting. The game provides textual, verbal, and nonverbal communication cues for the player to interpret and act on in a variety of contexts. The player is graded based upon the consequences reached as the result of his or her communications.

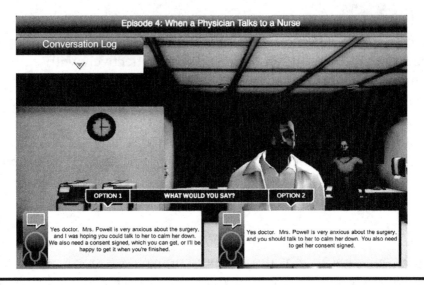

Figure 5.11   Screen shot from role-playing game "Communication Situation."

The player starts the game by choosing his or her character (i.e., a nurse or a physician). The player is then presented with a communication trigger, a situation that requires the player to initiate communication with another health care professional. The player must make an assessment of the situation and then initiate a communication event (e.g., a nurse call). The communication event determines how effective the player is at communicating the necessary information, according to the health care professional. A range of communication strategies is used to rate effectiveness, and the game reacts using a set of preprogrammed possibilities created based on input from focus groups of nurses and physicians.

A screen shot from "Communication Situation" is presented in Figure 5.11.

Data Mining Laboratory

Measuring and improving patient safety requires using data from a multitude of sources (Ballard 2015). During the final phase of the patient safety journey, health care delivery organizations should leverage technology to integrate and utilize large data sets. At BSWH, the DML applies advanced methods and software to integrate data from multiple organizational and regional databases. The DML also helps to look for trends in AE data and provides a wealth of information through the text mining of patient safety survey comments as well as the ability to drill into encounter-level data to provide valuable information on AEs or potential AEs.

Translating vast and complex clinical health data into actionable information resulting in evidence-based practices with improved safety and outcomes is its goal. The DML serves as a valuable resource to health care researchers.

BSWH supports continuous testing of basic research findings through institutional review board oversight, with a focus on disease prevention and treatment, and implements these strategies into the regional north-central Texas community.

Examples of DML projects and work include the following:

■ Provides trends in AE data and Patient Safety Survey comments
■ Compares of metrics across multiple health systems external to BSWH (e.g., the Dallas-Fort Worth Hospital Council) (Figure 5.12)
■ Uses the Dallas-Fort Worth Hospital Council Foundation data (or other similar external metrics) as a "trigger" for a focused, detailed, "deep dive" data analysis

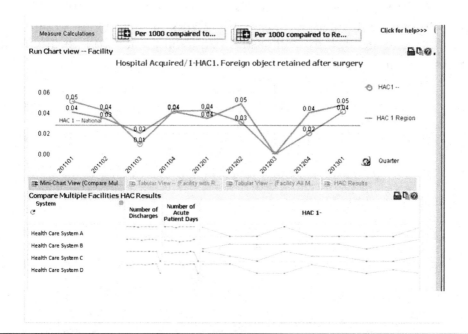

Figure 5.12 Patient safety benchmarking example: health care-acquired conditions (foreign object retained after surgery). (From http://www.dfwhcfoundation.org/data; as of July 8, 2013 5:20:09 pm.)

- Supported the Trauma Re-admissions Research Project for which the DML developed a predictive model of posttrauma readmissions for patients admitted to the trauma service over a one-year time span
- Conducts demonstrations of the DML concept and invites regional colleges and universities to attend with guest lectures and demonstrations; interactions involving the DML with faculty and students have been conducted with several universities

Conclusion

The journey to safer patient care depends on the leveraging of technology to assimilate and integrate patient safety data, standardize care processes and documentation, and improve communication and information exchange among care providers. Continually evolving technology enables health care organizations to better measure and analyze AEs, administer patient safety culture surveys across a variety of departments and facilities, use EHRs to reduce the potential for human error in patient care, and improve communication with novel approaches such as gaming technology. As the applications of HIT continue to grow and expand, the ability of health care organizations to leverage technology will assume an even greater role in driving and improving patient safety.

Conclusion

The BSWH commitment to patient safety is expressed in its vision "to be the most trusted name in giving and receiving safe, quality, compassionate health care," as well as its commitment to making care more STEEEP—safe, timely, effective, efficient, equitable, and patient centered. BSWH has more than 100 years of experience traveling the journey to safer care and ensuring that patient safety is a fundamental component of high-quality care.

To guarantee the highest levels of safe care while adapting to a health care environment that is changing ever more rapidly, organizations will need to rely not just on specific patient safety practices but also on a strong foundation for safe patient care. This foundation depends on the establishment of an organizational culture in which everyone is accountable for patient safety, the ongoing adoption and implementation of safety improvement processes that align with national priorities, and the innovative use of evolving HIT. With these components in place, organizations will be well positioned to proactively and continuously improve patient safety and prioritize safe care as a core element of their mission and business objectives.

Glossary

AE: adverse event

AHRQ: Agency for Healthcare Research and Quality

AMGA: American Medical Group Association

AMI: acute myocardial infarction

APPSS: Attitudes and Practices of Patient Safety Survey

ASPIRE: Achieving Synergy in Practice through Impact, Relationships, and Evidence

BAEMT: Baylor Adverse Event Measurement Tool

BCMA: Bar Code Medication Administration

BHCS: Baylor Health Care System

BSWH: Baylor Scott & White Health

CAUTI: catheter-associated urinary tract infection

CDAT: Clinical Data Access Team

CDC: Centers for Disease Control and Prevention

CLABSI: central line-associated bloodstream infection

CMO: chief medical officer

CMS: Centers for Medicare and Medicaid Services

CNO: chief nursing officer

COPD: chronic obstructive pulmonary disease

CRM: clinical risk management

CUSP: Comprehensive Unit-Based Safety Program

DML: Data Mining Laboratory

ED: emergency department

EHR: electronic health record

GTT: Global Trigger Tool

HAC: hospital-acquired condition

HAI: health care-associated infection

HCI: health care improvement
HIM: health information manager
HIT: health information technology
HSMR: hospital-standardized mortality ratio
HTPN: HealthTexas Provider Network
ICU: intensive care unit
IHI: Institute for Healthcare Improvement
IOM: Institute of Medicine
IS: information services
ISO: International Organization of Standardization
IT: information technology
IV: intravenous
MAR: medication administration record
MDRO: Multi-Drug-Resistant Organism Transmission
MEC: Medical Executive Committee
NDNQI: National Database of Nursing Quality Indicators
NPSG: National Patient Safety Goal
OPS: Office of Patient Safety
OR: operating room
PDCA: plan, do, check, act
PNE: pneumonia
POA: present on admission
POCMA: Phase of Care Mortality Analysis
PS: patient safety
PSI: patient safety indicator
PSL: patient safety liaison
PSO: patient safety officer
RCA: root cause analysis
REDI: role model, engage, direct, inform
RM: risk management
RRT: rapid response team
SBAR: situation, background, assessment, recommendation
SMART: specific, measureable, actionable, realistic, and time-bound
SME: subject matter expert
SMU: Southern Methodist University
SSI: surgical site infection
SSSL: Safe Surgery Saves Lives
STEEEP: safe, timely, effective, efficient, equitable, patient centered

STOP: Screening Tool for Oversedating Pharmaceuticals
SWH: Scott & White Healthcare
TIPS: Teamwork Improves Patient Safety
VAP: ventilator-associated pneumonia
WHO: World Health Organization

References

ABC News, *Your Three Words*. 2011. [cited August 27, 2015]; Available from: http://abcnews.go.com/US/words-live-event-good-morning-america/story?id=14469378.

Agency for Healthcare Research and Quality, *Morbidity and Mortality Rounds on the Web: A Troubling Amine*. 2006. [cited March 17, 2015]; Available from: http://webmm.ahrq.gov/case.aspx?caseID=136.

Agency for Healthcare Research and Quality, *Electronic Health Records*. 2014. [cited May 12, 2015]; Available from: http://healthit.ahrq.gov/ahrq-funded-projects/emerging-lessons/electronic-health-records.

Agency for Healthcare Research and Quality, *CUSP Toolkit*. 2015. [cited March 25, 2015]; Available from: http://www.ahrq.gov/professionals/education/curriculum-tools/cusptoolkit/index.html.

Ahmed, F. et al., Effect of influenza vaccination of healthcare personnel on morbidity and mortality among patients: Systematic review and grading of evidence. *Clin Infect Dis*, 2014. **58**(1): pp. 50–7.

Ballard, D.J., Indicators to improve clinical quality across an integrated health care system. *Int J Qual Health Care*, 2003. **15 Suppl 1**: pp. i13–23.

Ballard, D.J., *The Guide to Achieving STEEEP Health Care: Baylor Scott & White Health's Quality Improvement Journey*. 2015, Boca Raton, FL: CRC Press.

Ballard, D.J., B. Spreadbury, and R.S. Hopkins, 3rd, Health care quality improvement across the Baylor Health Care System: The first century. *Proc (Bayl Univ Med Cent)*, 2004. **17**(3): pp. 277–88.

Ballard, D.J. et al., *Achieving STEEEP Health Care*. 2014, Boca Raton, FL: CRC Press.

Berwick, D.M. et al., The 100,000 lives campaign: Setting a goal and a deadline for improving health care quality. *JAMA*, 2006. **295**(3): pp. 324–27.

Brennan, T.A. et al., Incidence of adverse events and negligence in hospitalized patients. Results of the Harvard Medical Practice Study I. *N Engl J Med*, 1991. **324**(6): pp. 370–76.

Carthey, J. and J. Clarke, *The "How To" Guide for Implementing Human Factors in Healthcare*. 2010. [cited March 7, 2015]; Available from: http://www.patientsafetyfirst.nhs.uk/ashx/Asset.ashx?path=/Intervention-support/Human+Factors+How-to+Guide+v1.2.pdf.

Centers for Medicare and Medicaid Services, *Decision Memo for Transcatheter Aortic Valve Replacement (TAVR) (CAG-00430N)*. 2012. [cited April 2, 2015]; Available from: http://www.cms.gov/medicare-coverage-database/details/nca -decision-memo.aspx?NCAId=257.

Centers for Disease Control and Prevention, *Hand Hygiene in Healthcare Settings*. 2015. [cited March 16, 2015]; Available from: http://www.cdc.gov/handhygiene /Basics.html.

Centers for Medicare and Medicaid Services, *The Official Web Site for the Medicare and Medicaid Electronic Health Records (EHR) Incentive Programs*. [cited May 12, 2015]; Available from: http://www.cms.gov/Regulations-and-Guidance/Legislation /EHRIncentivePrograms/index.html?redirect=/EHRIncentivePrograms/01 _Overview.asp.

Convery, P., C.E. Couch, and R. Luquire, Training physician and nursing leaders for performance improvement, in *From Front Office to Front Line: Essential Issues for Health Care Leaders*, S. Berman, Editor. 2012, Oakbrook Terrace, IL: The Joint Commission. pp. 59–85.

Corrigan, J.M. et al., *Crossing the Quality Chasm: A New Health System for the 21st Century*. 2001, Washington, DC: National Academy Press.

Graban, M., *"Stop the Line" in a Hospital*. 2009. [cited May 26, 2015]; Available from: http://www.leanblog.org/2009/03/stop-line-in-hospital/.

Graham, M.J. et al., Heuristic evaluation of infusion pumps: Implications for patient safety in Intensive Care Units. *Int J Med Inform*, 2004. **73**(11–12): pp. 771–79.

Guenter, P., New enteral connectors: Raising awareness. *Nutr Clin Pract*, 2014. **29**(5): pp. 612–14.

Haydar, Z. et al., Accelerating best care at Baylor Dallas. *Proc (Bayl Univ Med Cent)*, 2009. **22**(4): pp. 311–15.

Haynes, A.B. et al., A surgical safety checklist to reduce morbidity and mortality in a global population. *N Engl J Med*, 2009. **360**(5): pp. 491–99.

HealthIT.gov, *EHR Incentives and Certifications*. 2015. [cited May 12, 2015]; Available from: http://www.healthit.gov/providers-professionals/meaningful -use-definition-objectives.

Herrin, J., D. Nicewander, and D.J. Ballard, The effect of health care system admin- istrator pay-for-performance on quality of care. *Jt Comm J Qual Patient Saf*, 2008. **34**(11): pp. 646–54.

Hoonakker, P.L.T., P. Carayon, and J.M. Walker, Measurement of CPOE end-user satisfaction among ICU physicians and nurses. *Appl Clin Inform*, 2010. **1**(3): pp. 268–85.

Husch, M. et al., Insights from the sharp end of intravenous medication errors: Implications for infusion pump technology. *Qual Saf Health Care*, 2005. **14**(2): pp. 80–6.

Institute for Healthcare Improvement, *Conduct Patient Safety Leadership WalkRounds™*. 2015. [cited March 10, 2015]; Available from: http://www.ihi .org/resources/Pages/Changes/ConductPatientSafetyLeadershipWalkRounds .aspx.

Institute for Healthcare Improvement, *IHI Global Trigger Tool for Measuring Adverse Events*. 2015. [cited April 27, 2015]; Available from: http://www.ihi.org/resources/Pages/Tools/IHIGlobalTriggerToolforMeasuringAEs.aspx.

Institute for Safe Medication Practices. 2015. [cited April 7, 2015]; Available from: http://www.ismp.org/.

Institute of Medicine, *Patient Safety: Achieving a New Standard for Care*. 2004, Washington, DC: National Academy Press.

International Ergonomics Association, *Definition and Domains of Ergonomics*. 2015. [cited March 17, 2015]; Available from: http://www.iea.cc/whats/index.html.

The Joint Commission, *2010 Comprehensive Accreditation Manual for Hospitals: The Official Handbook*. 2009, Oak Brook, IL: Joint Commission Resources.

The Joint Commission, *National Patient Safety Goals*. 2015. [cited April 9, 2015]; Available from: http://www.jointcommission.org/standards_information/npsgs.aspx.

The Joint Commission, *Sentinel Event Alert: Safe Use of Opioids in Hospitals*. 2012. [cited March 26, 2015]; Available from: http://www.jointcommission.org/assets/1/18/SEA_49_opioids_8_2_12_final.pdf.

The Joint Commission, *Sentinel Event Data: Root Causes by Event Type, 2004—Q2, 2015*. [cited October 21, 2015]; Available from: http://www.jointcommission.org/assets/1/18/Root_Causes_Event_Type_2004-2Q_2015.pdf.

Kennerly, D. et al., Journey to no preventable risk: The Baylor Health Care System patient safety experience. *Am J Med Qual*, 2011. **26**(1): pp. 43–52.

Kennerly, D.A. et al., Description and evaluation of adaptations to the global trigger tool to enhance value to adverse event reduction efforts. *J Patient Saf*, 2013. **9**(2): pp. 87–95.

Kohn, L.T. et al., *To Err is Human: Building a Safer Health System: A Report from the Committee on Quality of Healthcare in America*. 1999, Washington, DC: National Academy Press.

Koppel, R. et al., Workarounds to barcode medication administration systems: Their occurrences, causes, and threats to patient safety. *J Am Med Inform Assoc*, 2008. **15**(4): pp. 408–23.

Likourezos, A. et al., Physician and nurse satisfaction with an Electronic Medical Record system. *J Emerg Med*, 2004. **27**(4): pp. 419–24.

Magill, S.S. et al., Multistate point-prevalence survey of health care-associated infections. *N Engl J Med*, 2014. **370**(13): pp. 1198–208.

Mannahan, C.A., Different worlds: A cultural perspective on nurse–physician communication. *Nurs Clin North Am*, 2010. **45**(1): pp. 71–9.

Manojlovich, M. and B. DeCicco, Healthy work environments, nurse–physician communication, and patients' outcomes. *Am J Crit Care*, 2007. **16**(6): pp. 536–43.

Nemeth, C. et al., Between choice and chance: The role of human factors in acute care equipment decisions. *J Patient Saf*, 2009. **5**(2): pp. 114–21.

Otieno, O.G. et al., Nurses' views on the use, quality and user satisfaction with electronic medical records: Questionnaire development. *J Adv Nurs*, 2007. **60**(2): pp. 209–19.

Poon, E.G. et al., Effect of bar-code technology on the safety of medication administration. *N Engl J Med*, 2010. **362**(18): pp. 1698–707.

Reason, J., Human error: Models and management. *BMJ*, 2000. **320**(7237): pp. 768–70.

Rosenstein, A.H. and M. O'Daniel, A survey of the impact of disruptive behaviors and communication defects on patient safety. *Jt Comm J Qual Patient Saf*, 2008. **34**(8): pp. 464–71.

Rothschild, J.M. et al., A controlled trial of smart infusion pumps to improve medication safety in critically ill patients. *Crit Care Med*, 2005. **33**(3): pp. 533–40.

Russ, A.L. et al., The science of human factors: Separating fact from fiction. *BMJ Qual Saf*, 2013. **22**(10): pp. 802–08.

Saleem, J.J. et al., Current challenges and opportunities for better integration of human factors research with development of clinical information systems. *Yearb Med Inform*, 2009: pp. 48–58.

Samore, M.H. et al., Surveillance of medical device-related hazards and adverse events in hospitalized patients. *JAMA*, 2004. **291**(3): pp. 325–34.

Shannon, F.L. et al., A method to evaluate cardiac surgery mortality: Phase of care mortality analysis. *Ann Thorac Surg*, 2012. **93**(1): pp. 36–43; discussion 43.

Slavin, K.E., American Nurses Association's best practices in seasonal influenza immunization campaign. *AAOHN J*, 2008. **56**(3): pp. 123–28.

Tannery, N.H. et al., Impact and user satisfaction of a clinical information portal embedded in an electronic health record. *Perspect Health Inf Manag*, 2011. **8**: p. 1d.

Weick, K.E. and K.M. Sutcliffe, *Managing the Unexpected—Assuring High Performance in an Age of Complexity*. 2001, San Francisco: Jossey-Bass.

Xiao, Y. and C.A. Probst, Engagement and macroergonomics: Using cognitive engineering to improve patient safety, in *Cognitive Systems Engineering in Health Care*, A.M. Bisantz, C.M. Burns, and R.J. Fairbanks, Editors. 2014, Boca Raton, FL: CRC Press. pp. 175–98.

Index

Printed in the United States
by Baker & Taylor Publisher Services